D0151287

Building Your Career

A GUIDE TO YOUR FUTURE

THIRD EDITION

Susan Jones Sears
THE OHIO STATE UNIVERSITY

Virginia N. Gordon
THE OHIO STATE UNIVERSITY

Prentice Hall

Upper Saddle River, New Jersey
Columbus, Ohio

Library of Congress Cataloging-in-Publication Data

Sears, Susan Jones.
    Building your career : a guide to your future / Susan Jones Sears, Virginia N. Gordon.—
3rd ed.
    Includes bibliographical references and index.
    ISBN 0-13-093105-5
      1. Career development. 2. Vocational guidance. 3. College students—Employment. I.
Gordon, Virginia N. II. Title.

HF5381 .S449 2002
650.14—dc21

2001033940

Vice President and Publisher: Jeffery W. Johnston
Acquisitions Editor: Sande Johnson
Assistant Editor: Cecilia Johnson
Production Editor: Holcomb Hathaway
Design Coordinator: Diane C. Lorenzo
Cover Designer: Thomas Borah
Cover Art: Artville
Production Manager: Pamela D. Bennett
Director of Marketing: Kevin Flanagan
Marketing Manager: Christina Quadhamer
Marketing Assistant: Barbara Koontz

This book was set in Times New Roman by Aerocraft Charter Art Service. It was printed and bound by Banta Book Group.
The cover was printed by Banta Book Group.

Pearson Education Ltd., *London*
Pearson Education Australia Pty. Limited, *Sydney*
Pearson Education Singapore Pte. Ltd.
Pearson Education North Asia Ltd., *Hong Kong*
Pearson Education Canada, Ltd., *Toronto*
Pearson Educación de Mexico, S.A. de C.V.
Pearson Education-Japan, *Tokyo*
Pearson Education Malaysia Pte. Ltd.
Pearson Education, *Upper Saddle River, New Jersey*

Copyright © 2002, 1998, 1995 by Pearson Education, Inc., Upper Saddle River, New Jersey 07458. All rights reserved. Printed in the United
States of America. This publication is protected by Copyright and permission should be obtained from the publisher prior to any prohibited reproduction, storage in a retrieval system, or transmission in any form or by any means, electronic, mechanical, photocopying, recording, or likewise. For information regarding permission(s), write to: Rights and Permissions Department.

10 9 8 7 6 5 4 3 2 1
ISBN 0-13-093105-5

To the memory of our loving mothers

THELMA L. JONES

IRMA K. NISWONGER

Contents

Three

What Do I Need to Know About Occupational Alternatives?   43

Four

What Do I Need to Know About Educational Alternatives?   63

Five

How Will I Decide?   83

Six How Will I Gain a Psychological Edge?   101

Seven
How Will I Advance My Career?   121

The Job Search and Resume Writing

Eight
Am I the Best Candidate?   147

Job Leads and the Job Interview

Nine

Where Do I Go from Here?   159

Preface

Planning and building a career is a lifelong process requiring a broad base of critical knowledge and skills. Individuals will have to draw upon this base many times as they explore, remain in, and change careers. Although some individuals plan ahead for effective career decisions, many others make career decisions only as the need arises—or even allow circumstances to dictate their careers, sometimes with less than satisfactory results.

This third edition of *Building Your Career* seeks to equip individuals with the knowledge, skills, attitudes, and behaviors required to make effective educational and career decisions. The book's detailed approach encourages self-assessment, imparts information about the work world of tomorrow, and helps readers explore academic and career alternatives pertaining to their interests and the careers they wish to pursue, now and in the future. Exercises are designed to involve the reader in career decision making for the present and the future. New to this edition are case studies in every chapter, which bring the discussion into the real world of work.

Chapter One begins by addressing some basic questions: How do people choose careers? Why do people work? What is a career? Why do I need to plan? The chapter explains the career choice process and personalizes it through six exercises designed to get readers started on their career journey.

Chapter Two explores personal characteristics as they relate to career interests, values, aptitudes, and skills. The exercises involve self-assessment of these characteristics.

Chapter Three enables students to identify, explore, and evaluate the various career options available to them and to consider how future trends might affect their career choices. The exercises help students narrow their options to general fields of interest and introduce informational interviewing to help them learn more about their choices from people working in those fields.

Chapter Four examines various educational options and college curricula. A matrix relates more than 100 college majors to associated interests and aptitudes.

Chapter Five pulls together the elements examined in previous chapters to formulate a perspective for decision making. A model of the decision-making process is suggested for students to use in examining their own decision-making style for everyday and important decisions alike.

Chapter Six examines the psychological edge identified with effective workers. It discusses how to acquire the knowledge and behavior associated with effectiveness, detailing specific strategies such as communicating effectively and managing stress. Included is the topic of ethical behavior and making ethical choices.

Chapters Seven and Eight leave behind the personal perspective of previous chapters and move on to the important tasks involved in the job search itself, encouraging students to take specific action steps each academic year to help them prepare for the job search later. Exercises in both chapters explore issues such as writing effective resumes and cover letters and interviewing for a job.

Chapter Nine helps students to pinpoint where they are in the career decision-making process and offers three methods by which to summarize the learning and accomplishments they have acquired during the course of this journey. This is a preamble to the next steps toward building satisfying careers, whatever the future may bring.

Acknowledgments

We would like to acknowledge Dr. Margie Bogenschutz, who provided helpful suggestions for the job-search part of this book. We also would like to thank all of the students who, in using this book, offered us valuable feedback about their diverse career planning needs. We have incorporated their suggestions in this new edition. We extend special thanks to Prentice Hall Editor Sande Johnson and Assistant Editor Cecilia Johnson, who guided us through the revision process.

How Do People Choose Careers?

Is there a magic formula for choosing a career? What are the factors involved? Some people think personal qualities, such as our interests and aptitudes or what we value, are the key factors in the process. These theorists recommend identifying our personal characteristics and matching them with compatible occupations. For example, a person who is excellent at math and enjoys the challenges and tasks associated with the field might explore math-related occupations such as engineering or accounting.

Other people think our family and socioeconomic background and even our heredity greatly influence career choices. Still others think our perceptions of who we are, or our self-concept, influence the occupational alternatives we consider. One widely accepted theory is that choosing a career is a part of our overall development as individuals. The developmental approach takes into account the different stages we pass through from childhood to mature adulthood. Developmentalists also suggest that each of us needs to learn how to manage career choice and career change over a lifetime.

Donald Super (1984), a developmental theorist, describes the many roles we assume at work and in life and how they emerge and interact across the life span. He contends that most of us play nine major roles in our lives: child, student, leisurite, citizen, worker, spouse, homemaker, parent, and retiree. These interacting roles constitute "career." Super identifies four principal theaters where we play out these roles: home, community, school, and the workplace. He believes that success in one arena facilitates success in another; difficulties in one are likely to lead to difficulties in another. Super contends that we must consider the interactions among all the roles as we focus on one (the worker role in this book). Exercise 1.1 asks you to identify the roles you are taking now and that you will take in the future.

EXERCISE 1.1   *Role Inventory*

List the three most important roles that you currently play (e.g., student, worker, sibling, friend):

1. _____

2. _____

3. _____

What three roles do you think will be most important to you in:

5 years?   10 years?

1. _____   1. _____

2. _____   2. _____

3. _____   3. _____

Do any of your current roles overlap or conflict? If so, which ones?

_____

When you picture yourself in the role of "worker," what images emerge?

_____

_____

_____

This book provides a road map through the maze of knowledge, skills, attitudes, and behaviors that are integral to career planning. Identifying and using these characteristics are critical in your overall career- and life-planning process.

Why Do People Work?

Most people work, at least in part, to earn a livelihood. Some people work for status, for the opportunity to be creative, or for the relationships work provides. Many people find their sense of identity through their work.

Attitudes toward work have a great impact on our aspirations and how we plan our lives. The quotes in Exercise 1.2 indicate the broad range of people's perceptions of work. They reflect philosophical, psychological, practical, and even negative views of work.

EXERCISE 1.2   *My Concept of Work*

Check three quotes below that best express your concept of work.*

_____   "A working person is a happy person."   *Unknown*

_____   "Never is there work without reward, nor reward without work being expended."
             Titus Livius

_____   "Work is love made visible."   *Kahlil Gibran*

_____   "That free men should be willing to work day after day, even after their vital needs
             are satisfied, and that work should be seen as a mark of uprightness and human

worth, is not only unparalleled in history but remains more or less incomprehensible to many people outside the Occident." *Eric Hoffer*

_____ "You can take this job and shove it—I ain't workin' here no more." *Popular song*

_____ "Without work all life goes rotten. But when work is soulless, life stifles and dies." *Albert Camus*

_____ "Work gives meaning to life." *Unknown*

_____ "Work is a four-letter word." *Unknown*

_____ "Self-actualizing people assimilate their work into their identity, into the self, i.e., work actually becomes part of the self, part of the individual's definition of him or herself." *Abraham Maslow*

_____ "Social development requires the assurance to everyone of the right to work and the free choice of employment." *United Nations Resolution #2542*

Write your personal definition of work.

_____

_____

How will your view of work affect the way you engage in the career-planning process?

_____

_____

_____

*Quotes are taken from *Career Planning and Decision Making* (Bloomington, IL: McKnight, 1979).

Your work strongly influences many aspects of your daily life, including your network of colleagues, your social status, and the types and amount of leisure activity you enjoy. Your career choice also determines the continuing education you will need, the supervision you will have, and the work culture in which you perform your job tasks. Table 1.1 illustrates some of the purposes of work.

Do any of these purposes agree with yours? Why did you select the ones you did? Work is important not only to individuals but to society as well. A society is usually stable when the majority of individuals work in relatively satisfying and productive occupations.

Purposes of work. **TABLE 1.1**

ECONOMIC	SOCIAL	PSYCHOLOGICAL
Ability to acquire physical assets such as property	Place to develop friendships	Self-identity
Ability to purchase goods and services	Sense of being needed by others	Sense of order in life
Evidence of success	Social status	Feeling of mastery or competence
	Achievement	Self-esteem
	Feeling of being valued	Feeling of belonging

Adapted from Herr & Cramer, *Career Guidance and Counseling Through the Life Span* (1992), New York: HarperCollins.

What Is A Career?

The concept of *work* is different from that of *career*. If you ask five people to define *career*, you probably will get five different responses. Many terms in the career development field are used interchangeably, although their meanings may vary. Several terms and their definitions follow. Are you using these definitions?

> *Career*—a continuous life process consisting of many work experiences and life roles
>
> *Vocation*—the work in which a person is regularly employed
>
> *Occupation*—an activity with a specific function in which one engages
>
> *Work*—an activity in which one does or performs something—paid or not paid
>
> *Job*—A work task or tasks for which the worker is paid
>
> *Position*—a group of tasks performed by one person

Many people use the terms *job* and *career* interchangeably, but they are different. Your career consists of your life history, which not only includes your vocation but, according to Donald Super, also includes the time you spend in school, in your community, and with your family. A job is one small part of your career. Career theorist David Tiedeman (1963) said, "Career is the imposition of direction in a person's vocational behavior, subject to his or her comprehension and will." Do you agree with these definitions? Do you equate *career* with *job?* This book will help you sort out the meanings of these terms as you engage in your lifelong career planning. Each decision you make will have an impact on every facet of your life, now and in the future.

Why Do I Need to Plan?

Planning a career is a process that begins early in life and continues throughout your lifetime. The extent of parental encouragement you received, the kind of toys you played with, the myriad experiences you engaged in, and the role models you were exposed to have influenced your perceptions of yourself and the kind of person you want to become. As you grew up, you probably created certain occupational fantasies; for example, you may have wanted to be a ballet dancer, a professional tennis player, or an astronaut. As you got older and knew yourself better, you then had additional ideas, perhaps more closely related to the reality of who you were. Your early fantasies, however, can reveal many truths about the kind of person you are now. Those fantasies also offer clues about your basic interests, values, and abilities. As you have thought about your career, you might have asked yourself some of these questions:

- What occupation did I want to pursue when I was in high school? What interests led me to that choice?
- What do I really want out of life?
- What occupations are best suited to the kind of person I am?
- What kind of lifestyle do I want?
- How will I know if my career decisions are good?
- In what area of study should I major?
- How much money will I need? How much can I make?
- Will I be able to balance my career with marriage and a family?
- Do I have what it takes to be a success? What does being successful mean to me?

These basic questions are what life and career planning are all about. Some people think they have little control over their future. Although we do not have total control over every facet of our lives, we *can* increase our odds of obtaining a satis-fying and productive career through careful planning. Exercise 1.3 asks you to evaluate your readiness to begin career planning.

Personal Factors   EXERCISE 1.3

Certain personal factors will affect how ready you are to begin the career planning process. Evaluate how the following personal factors might influence your readiness to engage in the exploration and decision-making tasks contained in this book. Mark the place along each continuum where you think you are today.

MOTIVATION. How motivated are you to spend the considerable time and energy required to be involved in the process of career planning?

◀ NOT VERY MOTIVATED   SOMEWHAT MOTIVATED   HIGHLY MOTIVATED ▶

RESPONSIBILITY. How able are you to take full responsibility for your involvement in the career-planning process and in your decisions, regardless of outcome?

◀ NOT VERY RESPONSIBLE   SOMEWHAT RESPONSIBLE   HIGHLY RESPONSIBLE ▶

COMPROMISE. How willing are you to examine (and possibly change) a strongly held belief or decision if it seems to be unrealistic or unattainable when new information indicates that a compromise is necessary?

◀ DIFFICULT TO COMPROMISE   DIFFICULT SOMETIMES   COMPROMISE EASILY ▶

COMMITMENT. How able are you to commit to a decision once you are convinced it is the best one at the time?

◀ NOT VERY COMMITTED   DIFFICULT SOMETIMES   HIGHLY COMMITTED ▶

Do you anticipate any problems associated with the personal factors above? Which ones, and how might you be influenced?

_____
_____
_____
_____

What other personal factors or attitudes might influence your readiness to begin the career planning process?

_____
_____
_____
_____

What Are Some Barriers to Career Choice?

Some beliefs about careers prevail in our culture, and certain attitudes thus are perpetuated. Examine these career beliefs:

> There is a perfect job for me if I can just find it.
>
> I can do any job that interests me as long as I am motivated and put forth the effort.
>
> Educational and vocational choices are the same.
>
> Most people wouldn't work if they didn't have to.
>
> Most people dislike their work.
>
> The younger people are when they choose a career, the better off they are.
>
> People know when they've chosen the right work because the job is fun.
>
> Certain jobs are best suited for men and certain jobs are best suited for women.
>
> Others know more about me than I do, so they will make a better career choice for me.
>
> Choosing an occupation is a once-in-a-lifetime decision, so it should be the right one.

Although a few of these statements possibly contain a kernel of truth, most experts agree that these statements are essentially false. In fact, some of these beliefs are unrealistic and may impede your progress through the career-planning process. Check out your beliefs and ask yourself, "Will any of my beliefs prevent me from taking certain courses of action or considering certain occupational areas?" If so, discuss your beliefs with your instructor, classmates, friends, and family.

Other barriers, too, can prevent you from making satisfying and timely career choices. Here are a few that could impede your career exploration.

You may feel pressured to make a specific academic or occupational choice that family members, peers, or other important people in your life want you to make. If you agree with this choice, there is no problem. If you have different ideas about your interests and what is important to you, you should pursue these alternatives by actively gathering information about them. In this way, you'll have choices to compare with the original idea and later won't regret not having explored them.

You may not be ready to make a career decision because of procrastination, lack of motivation, apathy, laziness, or a preoccupation with important events in your life. Career exploration and planning take place over a lifetime. You have been doing it since you were a child and usually are engaged in some facet of the process regardless of whether you are aware of it. Although you may not be "ready," you can gather information for future reference anytime and anywhere. For example, you might talk to upper-class students and faculty about majors or to workers in specific jobs. Work and volunteer experiences also are useful sources of career information. Personal behaviors and traits such as procrastination and lack of motivation may be habits that require examination in other contexts as well as in career planning.

You may not know how or where to begin the career exploration process. Because we think about our future throughout our lives, it is natural to continue to collect, weigh, and absorb information that we can use eventually in the career decision-making process. Consulting with a career counselor or an academic adviser may be a place to begin if this seems like a barrier to taking action.

You might be so anxious and overwhelmed with the prospect of beginning a search that you do nothing. If you are experiencing extreme anxiety when making academic or occupational choices, it may be helpful to consult a counselor. This is especially true if you have difficulty making decisions about other aspects of your life as well. In Exercise 1.4 you are to consider barriers to career planning on a personal level.

Overcoming Barriers

Can you think of other barriers that might impede the career exploration and decision-making process? If so, write them below:

_____

_____

_____

_____

What specific barriers do you think might have some effect on *your* progress in this area (e.g., career beliefs, lack of motivation, not knowing where to begin)?

_____

_____

_____

_____

What can you do to overcome these barriers now? In the future?

_____

_____

_____

_____

Where Do I Start?
The Career Choice Process

Career development takes place in numerous steps or stages. Table 1.2 outlines this process and its tasks.

Since every person has unique personal characteristics, matures at a different pace, and lives in a specific environment, career decision making becomes an individual life journey. Also, the type of work that interests you at age 18 may be quite different from what you want when you are 25 or 40. Every day, scores of people change careers. The need to be open-minded and flexible, therefore, is critical to negotiating your career-planning process successfully. The statements below are based on the model in Table 1.2. To help you determine where you are in the process, think about the statements below and check (✓) those that fit you best.

AWARENESS: I DON'T EVEN KNOW WHERE TO START!

_____ I feel pressured to make a decision.

_____ I'm not certain of my strengths and limitations.

_____ I'm not certain what is meant by knowledge, skills, attitudes, and behaviors.

_____ I'm not certain of the educational or occupational information I need or how to find it.

_____ I want other people to make decisions for me because I am not ready or capable.

TABLE 1.2   *The career planning process.*

PERSONAL CHARACTERISTICS	CAREER STAGES			
	Awareness (Chapter 1)	Exploration (Chapters 1–6)	Choice (Chapters 3–8)	Commitment (Chapters 7–9)
Knowledge	Is aware of the need for knowledge about self, work, and decision making; is aware of a process for deciding.	Gathers relevant information about self, educational, and occupational options; understands how career decisions are made.	Organizes and integrates knowledge about self, work, and decision making into a harmonious whole.	Knows how to make a commitment once decision is made.
Skills	Is aware that certain skills are needed to search and plan for a career.	Can find and use information about self and occupations; tries out decision-making skills.	Uses organizing, integrating, and decision-making skills.	Uses action-taking skills to implement decision.
Attitudes	Is aware of the need to identify work values and attitudes.	Clarifies work values and attitudes and compares with educational and occupational alternatives.	Incorporates and/or modifies attitudes into decision.	Decision is compatible with work values and attitudes.
Behaviors	Is aware there is an established personal pattern for making decisions.	Refines old deciding behaviors and tries new ones.	Makes a decision using effective decision-making behaviors (e.g., formulates an action plan).	Has taken specific actions to commit.

EXPLORATION: ALTHOUGH I KNOW IT WILL BE HARD WORK, I AM READY TO BEGIN THE INFORMATION-SEEKING PROCESS.

_____ I'm ready to assess my personal characteristics, including my interests, values, abilities, and overall personality.

_____ I need to gather and analyze information about educational options, occupations, and work environments.

_____ I'm ready to analyze how I approach the decision-making process and identify the skills I already have and those I still need to acquire.

_____ I'm ready to clarify honestly my attitudes toward work in general.

_____ I have not made a choice but am willing to *actively* explore.

CHOICE: I HAVE MADE A TENTATIVE DECISION BUT HAVE NOT DONE ANYTHING ABOUT IT.

_____ I have collected, organized, and integrated information about myself, occupations, and work into a harmonious whole.

_____ I have weighed carefully all the educational and occupational options I identified from the information I have gathered and analyzed.

_____ I have applied my decision-making skills to select the best option among the alternatives I considered.

_____ I am satisfied that my educational and vocational choices are realistic and reflect my personal values and goals.

COMMITMENT: I HAVE MADE A CHOICE AND TAKEN ACTION TO IMPLEMENT IT.

_____ I have developed a plan of action to implement my decisions.

_____ I'm planning for the future in an organized and realistic way.

_____ I'm aware that I probably will need to evaluate my decision and action plans periodically and change them when needed.

Although most people move consciously or subconsciously through these stages in the order given, they travel at different speeds and levels of understanding. You may have found statements in several stages that fit you. Even though we share common experiences, each of us will negotiate the process differently. You may be ready for the exploration phase. Another student may still need to learn about the factors involved in the decision-making process. Others may have to return to a previous stage to reconsider what they have found. For example, they may move back to the exploration stage if a specific choice turns out to be unrealistic or impossible; or once they are committed to creating an action plan, they may need to gather additional information.

Examine Table 1.2 again. Think about the knowledge, skills, attitudes, and behaviors needed within each stage. Then complete Exercise 1.5, to personalize that information.

My Place in the Career-Planning Process

EXERCISE 1.5

Place an X on the line below where you are now in the process of making career decisions.

| AWARENESS | EXPLORATION | CHOICE | COMMITMENT |

Why have you placed yourself in this phase of the career-planning process?

_____

_____

_____

_____

_____

This book will help you experience the career decision-making process as shown in Table 1.2, and also will help you understand the critical factors in making satisfying career and life decisions. As you read, you will learn more about what you will need to progress through the career-planning process and to commit to making specific choices. You will gather information about yourself in Chapter Two and information about occupational and educational options in Chapters Three and Four. Chapter Five covers decision making. Chapter Six presents some techniques for gaining a psychological edge both now and in the future. Chapters Seven and Eight will help you refine your job-search skills. In Chapter Nine you will be encouraged to review what you have learned and establish goals for your future.

The Career- and Life-Planning Checklist in Exercise 1.6 will give you a preview of what you will learn in this book as related to yourself.

My Career- and Life-Planning Checklist

The checklist below can help you think about the knowledge, skills, attitudes, and behaviors you will need to make effective educational and career decisions. The topics covered in the book are listed under the chapter in which they appear. Check (✓) the item you want or need to learn about, understand, and use as you engage in the career-planning process.

ONE: Getting Ready

awareness

_____ What is my attitude toward taking responsibility for my career planning?

_____ What does the career- and life-planning process mean? Where am I in the process, and how can I productively use this book?

_____ How should I progress through the decision-making process so I can make realistic and satisfying choices?

TWO: What Do I Need to Know About Myself?

exploration

_____ What are my perspectives on and attitudes toward work in general?

_____ What abilities do I currently possess for specific kinds of work tasks?

_____ What are my occupational interests?

_____ What is important to me in a job (e.g., income, type of people with whom I work, a job that allows me to be creative, to be self-employed)?

_____ How might my personality influence my occupational choices?

_____ How might my family background influence my occupational choices?

_____ How might my environment influence my career choices?

THREE: What Do I Need to Know About Occupational Alternatives?

_____ How can I locate the occupations that are realistic for me to explore? How can I narrow them down to a list of jobs that are realistic for me to explore?

exploration and choice

_____ How will changes in the future workforce affect me?

_____ Where can I find important information regarding specific occupations (e.g., salaries, necessary skills, educational requirements, physical requirements, employment trends)?

_____ What are the best sources for finding occupational information (e.g., Internet, printed, electronic, personal interviews)?

_____ What work skills will I need to acquire for employment in the 21st century?

_____ How can I evaluate and use occupational information once I have found it?

_____ How can I apply information about occupations to what I know about my own strengths and limitations?

_____ Where will future job growth and opportunities exist?

FOUR: What Do I Need to Know About Educational Alternatives?

_____ How can I select and/or confirm my choice of an academic major?

exploration and choice

_____ How do certain majors match my abilities and interests?

_____ What educational background will I need for certain occupations (e.g., apprenticeship, technical degree, two to four years of college, graduate degree)?

_____ What majors lead to specific occupational areas?

_____ Why don't certain occupations require specific college majors?

_____ How can I select courses to enhance the skills and knowledge I will need in the world of work?

_____ What can I do to test my ideas about a major (e.g., volunteer work, study abroad, experiential learning)?

FIVE: How Will I Decide?

_____ How can I learn to set short- and long-term personal, educational, and occupational goals?

_____ Why is my personal style of making decisions important?

_____ Where am I in the decision-making process?

_____ How can I learn effective career decision-making skills?

_____ How can I use information about self, occupational, and educational options to generate alternatives?

_____ How do I implement a career decision I have made?

_____ How do I periodically reevaluate my decisions?

exploration and choice

SIX: How Will I Gain a Psychological Edge?

_____ What does it mean to gain the psychological edge in life and in the workplace?

_____ What specific behaviors do personally effective individuals practice?

_____ How can I adapt to change effectively?

_____ How can I learn to communicate effectively with my peers, instructors, and co-workers?

_____ What stressors am I experiencing?

_____ How should I manage stress?

_____ How do I apply a personal "code of work ethics"?

exploration, choice, and commitment

SEVEN: How Will I Advance My Career? The Job Search and Resume Writing

_____ What are the advantages of starting now to compile information about my experiences?

_____ What job-search skills do I need to learn now?

_____ How should I write a resume that will appeal to a prospective employer?

_____ How should I write an effective cover letter?

_____ How do I stay current on how to send resumes electronically?

choice to commitment

EIGHT: Am I the Best Candidate? Job Leads and the Job Interview

_____ How can I generate job leads?

_____ What is the best way to prepare for a job interview?

_____ How can I make a good impression on a prospective employer during a job interview?

_____ What do I need to know about the difference between lawful and unlawful questions?

choice to commitment

_____ Where do I learn about cyber-interviews and other electronic methods?

_____ How should I follow up after an interview?

NINE: Where Do I Go from Here?

_____ Where am I now?

commitment   _____ What are my next steps?

After completing the readings and exercises in this book, you can monitor your progress by comparing the items you checked above with the items you will check in the last section of this book.

CASE STUDY   *Jed and Maria*

AWARENESS Jed is a first-year student at a moderately large college. He knows that eventually he will need to make a decision about a major, but doesn't feel strongly about any field. He feels frustrated, as he senses that his parents want him to make firm academic and career decisions soon. They have encouraged him to think about engineering because he seems to have a talent for math and science. Jed doesn't know much about engineering and is not sure he has the ability or motivation to pursue the difficult curriculum in this area.

His academic advisor has encouraged him to take a career course that is being offered, and Jed has agreed. He hopes that by exploring different career fields in an organized, systematic way, he will discover what might be compatible with his interests and abilities.

Maria has worked as a secretary in a high-tech firm since graduating from high school. Even though she completed a college preparatory track in high school, she didn't go on to college because she thought it would be too much of a financial drain on her family. No one else had gone to college in her family, and it seemed like a difficult goal to attain.

As a worker, Maria has been quite successful. Fortunately, she has a competent supervisor who was quick to recognize her skills. Even though most of Maria's duties remain clerical, she has been encouraged to expand the scope of her work. She has discovered that she is quite good with computers. She is able to spend a couple of hours a day working alongside a computer programmer and is learning programming language. Her company has a college tuition reimbursement program that she has decided to explore.

Maria was divorced recently and is highly interested in improving her earning capacity so she will be able to take care of her young daughter. Maria has decided to take a career-planning course at her local community college to help her gather information and focus on making a timely decision.

Summary Checklist

What I have learned

_____ Career planning is a lifelong process that began in childhood and will continue the rest of my life.

_____ My role as worker is one of many roles I play in life and is both separate and interwoven into the others; my concept of work reflects my attitudes and values toward my role as worker.

_____ Through the "Career- and Life-Planning Checklist," I have stated specific goals I want to accomplish in this course.

How I can use it

I can relax and feel confident that, by engaging in the process outlined in this text, I will be able to make an educational and/or career decision that will be satisfying for _this time in my life._

If you are using this book in a course, you will have the opportunity to discuss all aspects of the career-planning process. If you are using this book for self-study, obtaining the services of a career counselor can be invaluable. You are the one who needs to take full responsibility for your future career—after all, you are the one who will live it!

What Do I Need to Know About Myself?

Exploring the Self

In today's world, you may be wise to be less concerned with making *initial* occupational choices and more concerned with planning a career path that will involve a *series* of occupations. Studies suggest that most people hold six to nine jobs before they retire. The occupations they choose, however, probably will remain in a cluster or core area. For example, if you graduate from college with a degree in accounting, you might start out as an accountant in a large firm, move to supervising other accountants, become involved in training new accountants, quit the firm and start your own business, and, finally, teach accounting at a technical college. Along the way, you would have engaged in several occupations and continued to develop and enhance your core accounting skills.

Occasionally, individuals search for the "one best choice." They apparently believe there is only "one right occupation" for them and spend a great deal of time and energy trying to narrow down or discover their dream job. It is more useful in the early stages, however, to take a broad perspective and look for a family or group of occupations that seems appealing—and then explore several possibilities within that cluster.

Career development is a process that includes choosing, entering, adjusting to, and advancing in an occupation. As discussed in Chapter One, it is a lifelong process that interacts dynamically with your other life roles as well as with your environment. In this chapter you will gather information about yourself—personality traits, interests, values, aptitudes, and skills— and about influences in your environment, such as socioeconomic class, family patterns, and occupational stereotyping. Reflect upon this information as you develop plans for the future.

Personality Traits

Personality is a vital part of career decision making. A general definition of personality is "a collection of qualities or traits that are somewhat stable across situations." For example, if you are outgoing and assertive with your friends, you probably will be outgoing and assertive with your colleagues at work. Your personality also can be influenced by your environment. If you are outgoing and assertive and work in an environment where you are not permitted to express your personality, you may have to tone down your vivaciousness, and consequently be unhappy at work because you are not able to be yourself.

Certain personality characteristics are important in career decision making. For example, the gregarious person might do better as a politician or a sales representative than would a more quiet, shy person. Professional counselors, who try to help people in distress, must be able to demonstrate warmth and caring. Although personality is important, keep in mind that most occupations accommodate a variety of personality characteristics.

Holland's Personality Types

Knowing more about your personality can be helpful. It increases your self-awareness and may help you to identify preferred work environments. John Holland, a well-known career theorist, views personality type as the major influence in career choice and development. Holland believes that the choice of an occupation is an expression of personality and that the members of an occupational group have similar personalities. He also maintains that occupational achievement, stability, and satisfaction depend on congruence between personality and the work environment (Holland, 1985). Exercise 2.1 will help you discover how Holland's personality types relate to you.

EXERCISE 2.1 *Fitting Into Holland's Personality Types*

Holland suggests most persons can be categorized as one of six personality types: realistic, investigative, artistic, social, enterprising, or conventional. Look at the descriptions of Holland's personality types below and check (✓) the descriptors that best fit you.

REALISTIC

_____ Practical

_____ Frank

_____ Persistent

_____ Conservative

_____ Do not like to express feelings

SOCIAL

_____ Persuasive

_____ Insightful

_____ Extroverted

_____ Helpful

_____ Enthusiastic

INVESTIGATIVE

_____ Achieving

_____ Independent

_____ Curious

_____ Reserved

_____ Planful

ENTERPRISING

_____ Dominant

_____ Adventurous

_____ Persuasive

_____ Energetic

_____ Sociable

ARTISTIC

_____ Imaginative

_____ Sensitive

_____ Open

_____ Creative

_____ Expressive

CONVENTIONAL

_____ Responsible

_____ Conforming

_____ Orderly

_____ Cautious

_____ Practical

Most people are a combination of these six types but feel at home with two or three in particular. Add up your checkmarks for each type and then write the names of the three personality types in which most of your checkmarks appeared:

1. _____   2. _____   3. _____

Holland suggests that all occupations in the world can be divided into six work environments using the same descriptors as his personality types (realistic, investigative, social, enterprising, artistic, conventional). For example, business work environments often attract individuals with enterprising or conventional personalities, depending on the work tasks demanded in that specific work environment. Holland believes that most people are happiest in work environments congruent with their personality types. Examples of occupations in each of Holland's six work environments appear below.

REALISTIC	INVESTIGATIVE	SOCIAL
Mechanical engineer	Chemist	Social worker
Vocational agriculture teacher	Pharmacist	Nurse
Air traffic controller	Computer programmer	Counselor
Designer	Mathematician	History teacher
Chef	Veterinarian	Economist

ENTERPRISING	ARTISTIC	CONVENTIONAL
Banker	Artist	Accountant
Lawyer	Interior decorator	Finance expert
Personnel manager	Editor	Payroll clerk
Radio/TV announcer	Musician	Credit manager
Recreation director	Public relations expert	Secretary

To explore Holland's ideas more fully, ask your instructor or counselor for the Self-Directed Search, available from Psychological Assessment Resources, Inc., PO Box 990, Odessa, Florida 33556.

Other Personality Types

A second widely used approach to understanding personality is based on Carl Jung's views about perception, judgment, and attitude in human personality. Jung was a noted Swiss psychiatrist who developed a theory to explain human personality. He claimed that differences in behavior are the result of personality preferences. These preferences emerge early in life and form the foundation of our personalities. Jung believed these preferences explain our attractions and aversions to people, tasks, and events throughout our lives.

Jung's works were first translated to English in 1923. In 1942 Katharine Briggs, even before encountering Jung's writings, developed her own system of classifying people's behavior. She saw a great similarity between her own classification system and that of Jung. Briggs then became a student of Jung's writings and continued her quest to better understand human behavior. With the help of her daughter, Isabel Briggs Myers, Briggs began to develop and validate questions to measure personality differences. The result was the Myers-Briggs Type Indicator® (MBTI), published in 1956 by Educational Testing Service in Princeton, New Jersey. Since its publication, the MBTI has been widely used as a measure of individual differences.

As we mentioned, Jung believed that differences in behavior are the result of personality preferences. These preferences reflect both genetic predispositions and the influence of your early environment. Following are the four pairs of preferences according to Jungian theory:

Extroverted	or	Introverted
Sensing	or	Intuitive
Thinking	or	Feeling
Judging	or	Perceiving

EXTROVERTED OR INTROVERTED.   Jung theorized that people have one of two attitudes toward the world: *extroversion* or *introversion*. For people with an *extroverted* attitude, attention *"flows out"* and focuses on objects and people in the environment. They prefer to "act on the environment"—to change it and/or improve it. Extroverts try to create a life of activity, social contacts, and a wide circle of acquaintances (Lawrence, 1979).

For people with an *introverted* attitude, attention or energy is consolidated within. Introverts like to create a life with enough time for contemplation; they prefer to socialize with a few intimate friends (Lawrence, 1979). Privacy, as well as independent and introspective time, are important.

SENSING OR INTUITIVE.   According to Jung, there are two ways of perceiving or gathering data about the world: *sensing* and *intuition*. In *sensing,* you use your eyes, ears, and other senses to tell you what exists. Sensing is useful for gathering facts about a situation (as you are doing while reading this chapter).

Intuition is an indirect means of gathering data, characterized by ideas or meanings that bubble up from the unconscious, for example, a hunch. Intuition allows you to perceive meanings, symbols, and possibilities that go beyond the senses (Myers, 1980). Although these two dimensions are opposites, we all use both. Most of us have a preference, however, for one or the other.

The more you use your preferred processes, the more you continue to develop them (practice makes perfect).

FEELING OR THINKING.   *Thinking* and *feeling* are opposite ways of *making decisions.* If you use *thinking* when you are deciding, you tend to predict the logical result of any particular action you may take. Using thinking as a preferred mode of deciding means you are interested in causes, effects, and facts.

The other way to decide is through feeling. If you prefer to use *feeling,* you pay attention to anything that matters or is important to you or others (even if it isn't logical). You probably make decisions on the basis of personal values rather than solely on facts (Myers, 1980). Again, we all use both methods of deciding, but each of us has a preference for one or the other.

PERCEIVING OR JUDGING.   The fourth and final preference according to proponents of Jung's ideas is the use of *perception* or *judgment* in dealing with the outside world.

People with a judging attitude use thinking or feeling in their dealings with the world. *Judging* types are usually orderly and like everything in its place. They prefer to plan their lives and then follow the plan. They like to work things through to completion and to control events around them.

People with a *perceptive* attitude are those who rely mainly on sensing or intuition in dealing with the outside world. Perceivers are not particularly interested in neatness and order, but instead enjoy spontaneity. They do not like strict schedules and tend to keep their options open. Perceptive types may enjoy understanding events, but have relatively little interest in controlling them (Myers, 1980).

By identifying your preferences (*extroverted* or *introverted, sensing* or *intuitive, feeling* or *thinking,* and *judging* or *perceiving*), it is possible to get some idea of your personality "type." For example, an introverted, intuitive, thinking, and perceiving individual would be an INTP. The next exercise will give you some indication of your preferences.

*Personality Types** EXERCISE 2.2

Check (✓) all the adjectives that describe the behavior you use most often and answer the questions below.

EXTROVERSION

_____ Social

_____ Outspoken

_____ Communicate easily

_____ Rely on environment for stimulation

_____ Action-oriented

INTROVERSION

_____ Thoughtful

_____ Detached

_____ Unaware of surroundings

_____ Interest in ideas

_____ Prefer working alone or with a few people

SENSING

_____ Realistic

_____ Practical

_____ Observant

_____ Fun-loving

_____ Good at facts

INTUITION

_____ See new possibilities/solutions

_____ Value imagination

_____ Good at new ideas

_____ Good problem solver

_____ See relationships between ideas and theories

THINKING

_____ Logical

_____ Objective

_____ Consistent

_____ Analytical

_____ Give weight to facts

FEELING

_____ Sympathetic

_____ Appreciative

_____ Tactful

_____ Give weight to personal values

_____ Skillful in dealing with people

JUDGMENT

_____ Planful

_____ Decisive

PERCEPTION

_____ Imaginative

_____ Open to new ideas

_____ Orderly   _____ Flexible

_____ Stable   _____ Spontaneous

_____ Responsible   _____ Curious

Which patterns describe you better: Extroverted or Introverted? _____

Sensing or Intuitive? _____   Feeling or Thinking? _____

Perceiving or Judging? _____

What type (ESFP, ENTP, etc.) are you? _____

Keep in mind your type as you read about personalities and occupations.

Personality and Occupational Choices

Myers & McCaulley (1985) have speculated about the occupations particular types may enjoy most. Their ideas were used in developing the summary presented below.

PERSONALITY AND OCCUPATIONS

ISTJ	ISFJ	INFJ	INTJ
school administrator	nurse	minister	lawyer
dentist	preschool teacher	physician	biologist
detective	lab technician	English teacher	professor
ISTP	ISFP	INFP	INTP
farmer	dental assistant	psychiatrist	writer
engineer	mechanic	editor	artist
dental hygienist	bookkeeper	musician	social scientist
ESTP	ESFP	ENFP	ENTP
manager	coach	counselor	photographer
auditor	child care worker	drama teacher	journalist
salesperson	receptionist	entertainers	computer system analyst
ESTJ	ESFJ	ENFJ	ENTJ
surgeon	nurse	writer	lawyer
lawyer	secretary	consultant	scientist
factory supervisor	home economist	entertainers	mortgage broker

Do any of the occupations listed under your type interest you? If so, which ones?

_____

Did you notice that some occupations were listed more than once (e.g., lawyer, entertainer, writer)? This serves as an important reminder that while the personality is important in career decision making, it is only one of several influences. Regardless of your personality type, you may be successful in a wide range of occupations.

Now that you have spent time thinking about your personality traits, write several sentences that describe them. Focus on how these traits might influence your career path and career choices.

_____

_____

_____

_____

_____

_____

_____

_____

*This exercise is in no way related to or representative of the MBTI. For more information about the MBTI, ask your instructor, or write to Consulting Psychologists Press, Inc., 3803 E. Bayshore Rd., Palo Alto, CA 94303 or call them at 800/624-1765.

Use information about your traits as you try to identify work environments compatible with your personality. Keep in mind that personality alone will not predict if you will be satisfied in a particular occupational area.

Interests

Interests can be defined as things that hold one's attention or arouse one's curiosity. Interests are a person's likes and dislikes and are characterized by the person's intensity of feeling about a subject or thing. The level of intensity may range from a mild interest to an almost passionate interest.

Interests are learned—from your parents, in school, from friends, and from your life experiences. For example, when you engage in various activities, you react with specific feelings or attitudes. You like or dislike the activities, you feel challenged or bored, and you feel competent or clumsy. These personal reactions plus the feedback you receive on your performance (e.g., "You're really good at that") help to shape and focus your interests. You develop many interests during childhood and adolescence, and you continue to acquire interests throughout your life.

Interests can change. As we experience life and meet more people, we become interested in new things and discard some of our old interests. We also develop more complex thinking and understanding processes, and we may even seek new interests or activities with the hope of improving ourselves and making life more exciting.

Over the last two decades, interests have become the most important factor in measures of occupational selection. Most of us would like to work at something we enjoy. Career interest inventories have been developed to help identify interests and relate them to occupations. Interest inventories tally rankings for specific occupational preferences. By measuring the interests of successful and satisfied people in an occupation, researchers have developed scales that compare the interests of these individuals to the interests of people who are uncertain about what they want to do. These occupational scales are effective in predicting occupational satisfaction. For example, Table 2.1 shows the occupational scales of the Kuder Occupational Interest Survey and the California Occupational Preference Survey (COPS).

If your scores on the Kuder Occupational Interest Survey were to show a high correlation on the outdoor and mechanical scales, your job interests might be well suited to those of a forest ranger or park manager. Contact the counselors at your college or university to see what inventories are available. Libraries often are good career resources, too.

TABLE 2.1   *Occupational scales from Kuder and COPS.*

KUDER OCCUPATIONAL INTEREST SURVEY	CALIFORNIA OCCUPATIONAL PREFERENCE SURVEY (COPS)
Outdoor	Consumer Economics
Mechanical	Outdoor
Computational	Clerical
Scientific	Communication
Persuasive	Science–Professional
Artistic	Science–Skilled
Literary	Technology–Professional
Musical	Technology–Skilled
Social Service	Business–Professional
Clerical	Business–Skilled
	Arts–Professional
	Arts–Skilled
	Service–Professional
	Service–Skilled

Exercise 2.3 is a career interest inventory that we have designed to help you pinpoint your interests. It is based on 12 career areas identified by the U. S. Department of Labor.

EXERCISE 2.3   *Exploring Career Interests*

Read the following career interest inventory and indicate in the blank space whether you feel (L) low, (A) average, or (H) high interest in that area.*

INTEREST AREAS

_____ 01 ARTISTIC: Interest in creative expression of feelings or ideas

Workers in the Artistic Area use their special creative talents to express their ideas and feelings through art. They may express themselves through the creative use of words or through paintings or sculptures. Some workers in the Artistic Area may make and decorate products or perform before audiences on stage, on television, or in movies.

_____ 02 SCIENTIFIC: Interest in collecting and examining data about the natural world and applying them to problems in physical, life, or medical science

Workers in the Scientific Area do research on living and nonliving things. Scientists seek to expand and apply knowledge. They conduct experiments under controlled conditions. Some scientists test theories or discover new ways of explaining or doing things, while others develop useful ways of applying research and solving problems.

_____ 03 PLANTS AND ANIMALS (NATURE): Interest involving the physical care of plants and animals, usually in an outdoor setting

*Based on career areas identified by U. S. Department of Labor.

Occupations in the Plants and Animals Area include farming, forestry, and fishing. Farming involves planting and harvesting crops or raising livestock or poultry. Forestry involves planting, cultivating, and harvesting trees. Work settings for forestry include state and national parks, where wildlife and plants are protected. In landscape nurseries and gardens, shrubs and houseplants are raised to sell. Fishing activities include catching fish for commercial use and raising fish in hatcheries.

————— 04 PROTECTIVE (AUTHORITY): Interest in using authority to protect people and property

In the Protective Area, workers enforce laws, regulations, policies, and standards. They guard people and property. Some jobs in this area involve adventure and excitement. Workers such as police officers and fire fighters often face danger. Some workers, such as fire inspectors and security guards, try to prevent laws from being broken or crimes from being committed.

————— 05 MECHANICAL: Interest in applying mechanical principles to practical situations, using machines, hand tools, or techniques

Mechanical Area workers use tools and machines or apply the ideas and principles of machines and tools in their jobs. Workers in this area may be highly skilled, such as engineers, or they may operate simple machines.

————— 06 INDUSTRIAL: Interest in repetitive, concrete, organized activities in a factory setting

Since many different products are involved, workers perform diverse duties. Some set up and operate machines. Others inspect, weigh, or sort products, or load and unload machines. This work can be routine.

————— 07 BUSINESS DETAIL: Interest in activities requiring accuracy and attention to details, primarily in an office setting

Workers in this area need to be well organized and accurate. Some work with office machines, keyboards, or filing systems. Others are responsible for data entry and accounting. Some workers hold supervisory positions. Others in this cluster deal with nonemployees and handle questions, orders, or claims.

————— 08 SELLING (PERSUASIVE): Interest in influencing others through sales and promotional techniques

Selling involves workers who use their powers of persuasion to sell products or services. These workers can combine selling with an interest in a particular field of knowledge. For example, a person with an interest in computers could sell them.

————— 09 ACCOMMODATING: Interest in catering to and serving the desires of others, usually on a one-to-one basis

In the Accommodating Cluster, workers can provide a variety of services to people. Their work involves being pleasant and helpful. They try to make people relax and enjoy themselves. Workers need to have a feeling of responsibility for the people they are helping or serving. Some workers in this cluster are concerned for others' safety. For example, flight attendants are responsible for the safety of airline passengers.

————— 10 HUMANITARIAN: Interest in helping others with their mental, spiritual, social, physical, or vocational concerns

The Humanitarian Cluster includes workers who help people with personal problems. The problems might be mental or emotional, spiritual, social, psychological, or vocational. Special knowledge and skills are needed to work with people and their problems at this level.

_____   11 SOCIAL/BUSINESS: Interest in communicating ideas and information

The Social/Business Cluster includes workers who engage in planning, directing, and managing the activities needed to organize and deliver programs and services. They have many business contacts with people and gain satisfaction from being recognized and appreciated by others for their work. They must use personal judgment when making decisions.

_____   12 PHYSICAL PERFORMING: Interest in using physical skills and strength to entertain an audience

The Physical Performing Cluster includes workers in athletics and sports. Workers may coach, officiate, or perform. They undergo rigid training periods and have to cope with mental pressures and physical risks. They seek recognition or appreciation from others.

MY SPECIFIC INTEREST AREAS

Write the names of the areas in which you are most interested.

1st choice: _____   3rd choice: _____

2nd choice: _____   4th choice: _____

Values

Values are your basic beliefs, the beliefs you hold most dear. They are a source of motivation that can be seen in your actions—in the attraction to or avoidance of the pursuit of "things" such as money, power, or spirituality. Some values hold more meaning than others. We tend to pursue more vigorously the values that have more meaning to us than we do the values with less importance to us. For example, "getting an education" must have a positive implication for you or you wouldn't be in college. How actively you pursue your education is related in part to the strength of your value.

Values sometimes conflict—fulfilling one interferes with achieving another. For example, you might value completing your education as soon as possible. At the same time, you might value owning a car. Thus, you may feel conflicted as you try to decide whether to use your money to buy a car or to pay tuition. You will encounter conflicts throughout life that will force you to rank your values, whether you are or are not aware of the choice.

Sometimes identifying your personal life values is difficult. One way of assessing your values is to examine choices you have made in the past. Exercises 2.4a and 2.4b will help you identify the values you utilized in your past choices.

EXERCISE 2.4a *Exploring Life Values*

1. What types of people did you choose to spend time with in high school? Why?

_____

_____

2. What types of leisure activities do you pursue? Why?

_____

_____

3. If you have purchased an automobile, which one did you choose and why?

_____

_____

4. If you have volunteered your time, what activities did you choose and why?

_____

_____

5. When you select friends now, what characteristics do you hope they will possess?

_____

_____

6. When you purchase clothes or other personal items, what guides your purchases? Why?

_____

_____

7. What are the three most important values guiding your life right now?

_____

_____

8. Have you been surprised by any of your responses to the first seven questions? Why or why not?

_____

_____

Because values motivate you to pursue or avoid an activity or state of mind, and thus are the foundation for your goals, they are extremely helpful in determining your present and future career directions. Assessing your work values is essential as you engage in career decision making. Exercise 2.4b will help you identify your current work values.

Exploring Work Values   EXERCISE 2.4b

Complete the work values inventory below. Circle the number that corresponds most closely to your values.

WORK VALUES	NOT VERY IMPORTANT		VERY IMPORTANT
1. *Variety:* Being involved in several activities; changing from one activity to another often; having new experiences.	1	2	3
2. *Accuracy:* Doing things in a correct and precise manner; being exact.	1	2	3

	1	2	3
3. *Independence:* Being free to make decisions and plans using your own personal judgment.	1	2	3
4. *Adventure:* Doing exciting things that often involve the unexpected, danger, or risk.	1	2	3
5. *Routine:* Doing something the same way each time.	1	2	3
6. *Interaction:* Being involved with people; sharing ideas; developing plans; being part of a group.	1	2	3
7. *Mechanical:* Working with things, objects, tools, and machines.	1	2	3
8. *Creativity:* Developing new things or ideas; doing things in a new way.	1	2	3
9. *Social:* Helping others and being concerned about their needs.	1	2	3
10. *Production:* Using your physical skills to work on or make things.	1	2	3
11. *Leadership:* Planning activities and managing the duties of others.	1	2	3
12. *Scientific:* Experimenting, testing, and trying things.	1	2	3
13. *Communications:* Presenting ideas through speaking or writing.	1	2	3
14. *Business:* Selling or promoting an idea, product, or service to people.	1	2	3
15. *Expression:* Interpreting and expressing feelings, ideas, and information.	1	2	3
16. *Influence:* Influencing the thinking and behavior of others by providing ideas and information to change their opinions and attitudes.	1	2	3
17. *Recognition:* Achieving acceptance, acknowledgment, appreciation, renown.	1	2	3
18. *Economic reward:* Receiving good pay, fringe benefits, and economic incentives.	1	2	3
19. *Prestige:* Performing work that provides standing in the eyes of others and evokes respect.	1	2	3
20. *Power:* Being in authority, directing others, and making important decisions.	1	2	3

What do you value that is *not* on the list?

_____

Which three work values are most important to you?

1. _____ 2. _____ 3. _____

Work values have been categorized into the following Career Areas. Find your three *most important* work values and circle them.

WORK VALUES BY CAREER INTEREST AREA

ARTISTIC	SCIENTIFIC	PLANTS AND ANIMALS	PROTECTIVE
recognition	independence	variety	independence
interaction	mechanical	independence	adventure
creativity	scientific	interaction	interaction
leadership	prestige		communications
communications	creativity		business
expression			
influence			

MECHANICAL	INDUSTRIAL	BUSINESS DETAIL	SELLING
accuracy	accuracy	accuracy	independence
independence	routine	interaction	interaction
routine	mechanical	mechanical	business
mechanical	production	business	
production			

ACCOMMODATING	HUMANITARIAN	SOCIAL/BUSINESS	PHYSICAL PERFORMING
independence	variety	variety	recognition
routine	independence	recognition	independence
interaction	interaction	independence	adventure
business	social	interaction	production
	influence	leadership	
		communications	
		business	
		influence	
		economic reward	
		prestige	

Aptitudes

The general aptitudes of individuals are usually broad enough for the average person to meet the requirements of several jobs. Nevertheless, important in career planning is that some occupations require specialized aptitudes or the potential to develop them. You may never have been called upon to perform activities or tasks that utilize a certain talent, so it remains undiscovered. Therefore, it is helpful for you to try out lots of activities to see which ones tap your skills. Exercise 2.5 provides descriptions of some generally accepted aptitude areas. Read each one carefully and begin to identify your strongest ones.

Exploring Aptitudes   EXERCISE 2.5

The definitions of aptitudes presented below are adapted from a list provided by the U. S. Department of Labor. Think about the definitions as you read them, and rate yourself in each area.

Aptitudes: Categories

MECHANICAL REASONING

Understanding how different kinds of mechanical objects work.

SPACE RELATIONS

Looking at flat (two-dimensional) drawings or pictures of objects and forming mental images of them in three dimensions—height, width, and depth. Picturing how objects would look if seen from different angles.

COMMUNICATION/VERBAL AND WRITTEN

Using the English language correctly to communicate and present ideas clearly. Being able to identify correct use of the English language.

SCIENTIFIC

General ability to reason and make judgments. Analytical and systematic.

SOCIAL

Able to work well with others, negotiate, and encourage.

MATH/COMPUTATIONAL

Performing basic math operations (e.g., addition, subtraction, multiplication).

CLERICAL SKILLS

Ability to follow directions and perform detailed clerical tasks quickly and accurately.

LEADING/TEACHING

Ability to persuade, influence, or motivate others to become involved.

MOTOR COORDINATION

Ability to coordinate eyes, hands, or fingers rapidly.

ARTISTIC/CREATIVE SKILLS

Ability to design or produce an art form, music, or drama. Inventing, designing, or developing new ideas.

Next, rate yourself by circling the number that represents your level on each of the aptitudes below. Compare yourself with others in your age group. Use school grades, work experiences, leisure activities, and others' opinions about your aptitudes to guide your self-rating.

Aptitudes: Self-Rating

	MECHANICAL REASONING	MATH/ COMPUTATIONAL	SPACE RELATIONS	SOCIAL	COMMUNICATION VERBAL AND WRITTEN
High	7	7	7	7	7
	6	6	6	6	6
	5	5	5	5	5
Average	4	4	4	4	4
	3	3	3	3	3
	2	2	2	2	2
Low	1	1	1	1	1

	LEADING/ TEACHING	SCIENTIFIC	MOTOR COORDINATION	CLERICAL SKILLS	ARTISTIC/CREATIVE SKILLS
High	7	7	7	7	7
	6	6	6	6	6
	5	5	5	5	5
Average	4	4	4	4	4
	3	3	3	3	3
	2	2	2	2	2
Low	1	1	1	1	1

List your three strongest aptitudes:

1. _____

2. _____

3. _____

As you can see below, aptitudes also can be grouped by interest areas. Circle your three strongest aptitudes in the 12 Career Areas that follow.

APTITUDES BY CAREER INTEREST AREA

ARTISTIC	SCIENTIFIC	PLANTS AND ANIMALS	PROTECTIVE
communication/written	communication/written	manual dexterity	scientific
manual dexterity	math/computational	communication/verbal	communication/verbal
artistic/creative	space relations	computational	motor coordination
motor coordination		clerical skills	
MECHANICAL	**INDUSTRIAL**	**BUSINESS DETAIL**	**SELLING**
communication/written	communication/written	communication/written	communication/verbal/written
math/computational	math/computational	manual dexterity	leading/teaching
space relations	space relations	space relations	math/computational
mechanical reasoning	manual dexterity	clerical skills	clerical skills
manual dexterity			social
ACCOMMODATING	**HUMANITARIAN**	**SOCIAL/BUSINESS**	**PHYSICAL PERFORMING**
communication/verbal	leading/teaching	communication/verbal	space relations
social	communication/verbal	communication/written	artistic/creative
manual dexterity	manual dexterity	math/computational	motor coordination
		leading/teaching	

Write the names of the Interest Areas that reflect both your interests and aptitudes:

_____

_____

In Chapter Four you will be able to translate the above information about your interests and aptitudes into college major possibilities. This will help you identify, confirm, or explore possible academic directions.

Skills

A skill is the ability to do something. You have many skills, some of which you probably take for granted. Sometimes you might be unsure of your skills and under-rate or minimize them. Most of us have difficulty if asked to recite our own skills. What about you? What is your strongest skill?

_____

_____

Skills may be natural abilities or they may be acquired through education and training. In college you acquire life skills (e.g., managing your money, maintaining your clothes, organizing your time), as well as skills to help you earn a living. What skills are you learning to help you earn your living?

_____

_____

_____

Transferable skills are those that can be utilized in several different occupations. For example, teaching in school and training sales workers both require instructional skills. Other examples of transferable skills are analyzing, negotiating, communicating, clarifying, and evaluating.

Work-content skills are often referred to as *functional skills*. Functional skills are competencies that enable you to perform the tasks required in specific occupations. Review the functional skills below and answer two questions:

1. Which skills do I currently possess?
2. Which skills do I want to develop?

Then complete Exercise 2.6a, in which you will identify your skills and associate them with specific occupations. Exercise 2.6b will help you to identify your skills by looking at your achievements.

EXERCISE 2.6a *Exploring Skills*

The list of words below identifies work skills associated with different occupations. Put a checkmark (✔) in front of those skills you currently possess.

I am able to:

_____ 1. express	_____ 18. rescue
_____ 2. create	_____ 19. confront others
_____ 3. entertain	_____ 20. prevent accidents
_____ 4. communicate	_____ 21. repair
_____ 5. visualize	_____ 22. drive
_____ 6. experiment	_____ 23. build
_____ 7. apply	_____ 24. maintain
_____ 8. solve	_____ 25. use technology
_____ 9. diagnose	_____ 26. load goods
_____ 10. analyze	_____ 27. inspect materials
_____ 11. work in natural environments (trees, parks, etc.)	_____ 28. manufacture
_____ 12. harvest	_____ 29. regulate products
_____ 13. groom	_____ 30. monitor people and data
_____ 14. care for plants	_____ 31. manage an office
_____ 15. care for animals	_____ 32. keyboard
_____ 16. protect others	_____ 33. perform accounting
_____ 17. guard property and people	_____ 34. classify objects or data
	_____ 35. budget

_____ 36. sell

_____ 37. influence others

_____ 38. provide service(s)

_____ 39. purchase

_____ 40. work with customers

_____ 41. deliver goods

_____ 42. assist others

_____ 43. comfort and please others

_____ 44. usher

_____ 45. work with people

_____ 46. counsel others

_____ 47. teach others information

_____ 48. rehabilitate

_____ 49. solve problems

_____ 50. provide spiritual guidance

_____ 51. lead others

_____ 52. respond to others

_____ 53. defend

_____ 54. organize

_____ 55. prepare

_____ 56. perform before an audience

_____ 57. play or perform sports

_____ 58. compete

_____ 59. officiate

_____ 60. coach

Count the number of checkmarks (✓s) in each of the categories below and write the totals in the blank spaces:

1–5 = _____ (Artistic)   6–10 = _____ (Scientific)

11–15 = _____ (Plants and Animals)   16–20 = _____ (Protective)

21–25 = _____ (Mechanical)   26–30 = _____ (Industrial)

31–35 = _____ (Business Detail)   36–40 = _____ (Selling)

41–45 = _____ (Accommodating)   46–50 = _____ (Humanitarian)

51–55 = _____ (Social/Business)   56–60 = _____ (Physical Performing)

WORK SKILLS

In which two of the 12 Career Areas did you have the most checkmarks?

_____ and _____

These are the two areas in which you currently have the most functional skills.

What skills do you most enjoy using? These may be the ones that motivate you.

_____

_____

_____

_____

What three skills that you don't have now would you like to acquire? Why?

_____

_____

_____

_____

Identifying Skills via Achievements

Analyzing your achievements also can help you identify your skills. Think about three achievements you have accomplished during the last three years. Achievements include projects you have completed, goals you have attained, and paid or unpaid jobs you have held. Write a brief description of your achievements and then indicate the skills you think led to your success. Use this example as your guide.

EXAMPLE OF AN ACHIEVEMENT

Megan is a 20-year-old college junior. The student education organization to which she belongs was having serious budget problems. Megan organized a conference called "Technology in Education" to raise money for the organization. Other students were enthusiastic about her ideas and wanted her to be the leader. Megan found a site for the conference, persuaded speakers to volunteer their services, designed a promotional brochure, and recruited a committee to publicize the conference. The conference was a huge success, raising $3,000. Evaluations from attendees indicated that it had been stimulating and well-organized.

SKILLS DISPLAYED

Megan demonstrated her skills in leading, organizing, persuading, persisting, problem solving, working with people, communicating, creating, and getting the job done.

Brief description of your achievement #1:

_____

_____

_____

Skills displayed:

_____

_____

_____

Brief description of your achievement #2:

_____

_____

_____

Skills displayed:

_____

_____

_____

Brief description of your achievement #3:

_____

_____

_____

Skills displayed:

_____

_____

_____

How are the skills you identified in analyzing your achievements similar to the functional skills you checked in Exercise 2.6a?

_____

_____

_____

Now, turn to the Career Plans at the end of the chapter and complete Individual Career Plan #1. Then answer the questions accompanying the Career Plan.

How Does My Environment Influence My Career Choices?

Career theorist John Krumboltz suggests that environmental factors influence career decision making. Since the early 1950s, sociologists have explored how career decisions are affected by social environment. Family and socioeconomic status, general economic conditions, society's stereotypes about specific occupations, and its attitudes about multicultural populations all influence career development.

Socioeconomic Status (SES)

Your social and economic background is related to your family's resources. You inherit from your parents certain financial and other resources that, to some extent, influence your career choices. Your family's financial status determines things such as where you live and what schools you attend. In turn, these can affect your values, occupational expectations, opportunities, and gender-role expectations. Because social status often is passed down from generation to generation, you may have benefited by being exposed to many opportunities or, on the other hand, you may not yet have had the opportunity to recognize all the career options open to you.

Even though your SES may have affected your career ideas so far, many career-related decisions lie ahead. High aspirations and motivation to achieve will help you reach your goals. In Exercise 2.7, indicate how your socioeconomic status has affected your career options and thinking.

Exploring Socioeconomic Status EXERCISE 2.7

Think about your family. How would you describe your socioeconomic level (lower, middle, upper)?

_____

How has your SES influenced which schools you have attended?

_____

_____

How has your family influenced your ideas about your career?

_____

_____

Family Influences

Additional aspects of your family background can be influential in career decision making. In studies of college students' career development, researchers have found that parents were the most influential career role models for students. Mothers seemed to exert the greatest influence during their children's high school years, and fathers seemed more influential in their college-aged children's decisions. Exercise 2.8 is designed to help you think about ways your family has influenced your career development.

EXERCISE 2.8 *A Career Genogram*

A genogram is a graphic representation of your biological and stepgrandparents, parents, aunts, uncles, and siblings. Complete the genogram to help you identify models who may have influenced your occupational perceptions, as well as the perceptions you have of yourself as a worker. You may need to talk with your parents or other relatives to complete this activity.

After you have completed your Career Genogram, answer the following questions:

1. Do any occupations show up repeatedly? If so, which ones?

   _____

2. Do any general career fields show up repeatedly (e.g., business, medicine)? If so, which ones?

   _____

3. What levels of socioeconomic status are reflected in your genogram (e.g., blue collar, white collar, professional)?

   _____

4. What were the attitudes toward work in your family (e.g., important, unimportant, enjoyable, not enjoyable)?

   _____

   _____

   _____

5. What were the work values in your family (e.g., independence, security, high salaries)?

   _____

   _____

   _____

6. What behaviors and attitudes were reinforced as they related to males and females?

   _____

   _____

7. Did both of your parents work outside the home? _____ Yes _____ No

   If they both worked, how did that influence you? If only one worked, how did that influence you?

   _____

   _____

   _____

GENOGRAM

Put the initials of family members in the parentheses below each relative (use stepparents/siblings when applicable), and write their occupations on the lines below, if known.

MATERNAL

Grandmother ( ) _____

Grandfather ( ) _____

Aunt ( ) _____

Uncle ( ) _____

MOTHER ( ) _____

Aunt ( ) _____

Uncle ( ) _____

Aunt ( ) _____

Cousin ( ) _____

Cousin ( ) _____

Cousin ( ) _____

Cousin ( ) _____

Cousin ( ) _____

PATERNAL

Grandmother ( ) _____

Grandfather ( ) _____

Uncle ( ) _____

Aunt ( ) _____

FATHER ( ) _____

Aunt ( ) _____

Uncle ( ) _____

Cousin ( ) _____

Cousin ( ) _____

Cousin ( ) _____

Cousin ( ) _____

Cousin ( ) _____

Sibling ( ) _____

Sibling ( ) _____

Sibling ( ) _____

Sibling ( ) _____

8. How did your parents and grandparents handle the multiple roles of worker, spouse, parent, and child?

_____

_____

_____

_____

9. What life role do you think your parents believe is most important for you (e.g., worker, spouse, parent, child, citizen)? Briefly explain your answer.

_____

_____

_____

_____

10. Do any family members have unfulfilled dreams they are trying to live vicariously through you? If so, who and how?

_____

_____

_____

_____

_____

11. As you think about your answers to these questions, what influence do you think your family has had on your career development and decision making?

_____

_____

_____

_____

_____

The Impact of Gender

Whether you are female or male has influenced some of the choices you have made, as well as some of the choices your parents made for you. For instance, gender might have influenced the toys you were given, whether you were encouraged to take risks, your high school curriculum, and, in some cases, your choice of academic major. Often gender-related messages are subtle and their influence is difficult to discern. For example, if three generations of women in your family have been homemakers and you are a woman considering an engineering career, your beliefs and attitudes about women who work outside the home may produce conflict in your career choice. Consider the "what ifs" by completing Exercise 2.9.

What If?

Take a few minutes to write a paragraph called "How My Life Would Be Different If I Were to Wake up Tomorrow as the Other Gender." Include comments about your family life, relationships with your parents, high school activities, high school courses, expectations of your family and friends, and possible occupational options.

_____

_____

_____

_____

_____

_____

_____

_____

_____

What themes are apparent in your life as the "opposite sex"?

_____

_____

_____

Are any surprising to you? If so, which ones?

_____

_____

_____

Occupational Stereotyping

You may hold stereotypes about certain occupations, which can also influence your career choices. Stereotypes come from beliefs that our society and our families have about different groups—females, males, African-Americans, Jews, Christians, senior citizens, etc. Stereotypes can result in inaccurate judgments about situations and people and hold you back from taking particular steps. For example, if you are a female and have been taught that only certain occupations are appropriate for women (e.g., nursing, teaching, clerical), then you may believe you have limited options.

Our society deems certain types of work appropriate to either men or women. Men are encouraged to explore a wide variety of occupations, yet the areas of child care and nursing are frequently seen as "off-limits" or "women's work." Women, on the other hand, are discouraged from seeking education and training in science and math-related occupations or in trades such as construction, manufacturing, and transportation. The effect of such stereotyping is that many females work at lower-paying occupations with fewer opportunities for advancement. Exercise 2.10 will help you identify your beliefs about occupations you have considered.

EXERCISE 2.10 *Occupational Options*

List the occupations you have ever considered and indicate by placing a checkmark (✓) if you think the occupation is appropriate for men, for women, or for both.

OCCUPATION	FOR MEN ONLY	FOR WOMEN ONLY	FOR BOTH
1.			
2.			
3.			
4.			
5.			
6.			
7.			
8.			
9.			

List the occupations next to which you checked "For Men Only" or "For Women Only" and give reasons for your decisions.

OCCUPATION	REASON WOMEN/MEN SHOULD *NOT* ENTER THE OCCUPATION
1.	
2.	
3.	
4.	
5.	

What are your conclusions after completing Exercises 2.9 and 2.10? Have you eliminated possible occupational options because of your gender or occupational stereotyping? If you answered "yes," keep an open mind as you complete the activities in this book. You will always have a chance to expand your occupational options.

Other Environmental Factors

We have discussed only a few of the environmental factors (SES, family background, occupational stereotyping) that can influence your career development. Other factors can be influential, too. For example, some researchers suggest that middle-class parents tend to value self-direction in their children, whereas parents with lower SES tend to value conformity. Self-direction and conformity are important characteristics and may be reflected in the choices we make as adults. Also, those who study child-rearing practices suggest that boys are more apt than girls to be encouraged to take risks and assert themselves. Do these implications lead to differences in career choices? As researchers continue to try to answer these questions, you can challenge your own thinking and examine your personal beliefs. Don't underestimate yourself.

Turn to Individual Career Plan #2 and summarize how your environment has influenced your ideas about a career choice.

Complete the summary profile below by circling the Career Areas that best reflect your answers in Exercises 2.1–2.6. Then summarize your views about personality by answering the questions following the chart. Which of these career interest areas best reflect your interests, work values, work aptitudes, and work skills?

Summary Profile

INTERESTS

Artistic	Protective	Business Detail	Humanitarian
Scientific	Mechanical	Selling	Social/Business
Plants and Animals	Industrial	Accommodating	Physical Performing

WORK VALUES

Artistic	Protective	Business Detail	Humanitarian
Scientific	Mechanical	Selling	Social/Business
Plants and Animals	Industrial	Accommodating	Physical Performing

WORK APTITUDES

Artistic	Protective	Business Detail	Humanitarian
Scientific	Mechanical	Selling	Social/Business
Plants and Animals	Industrial	Accommodating	Physical Performing

WORK SKILLS

Artistic	Protective	Business Detail	Humanitarian
Scientific	Mechanical	Selling	Social/Business
Plants and Animals	Industrial	Accommodating	Physical Performing

Looking at your Individual Career Plan, which two career interest areas seem congruent with your interests, preferred work activities, work values, and aptitudes?

1. _____

2. _____

You will be using these two areas to do further career exploration in Chapter Three.

Personality Traits

Review the sentences you wrote in Exercise 2.2 describing your personality traits. Is what you wrote compatible with the career interest areas you identified in the previous step? If so, how?

_____

_____

If not, do you have career interest areas with which your description is compatible? Which ones?

_____

_____

INDIVIDUAL CAREER PLAN #2

Summary of Environmental Influences on My Career Development

SOCIOECONOMIC STATUS

Briefly summarize how your socioeconomic status has influenced your career decision making:

_____

_____

_____

_____

_____

FAMILY BACKGROUND

Briefly summarize how your family's occupational choices, work attitudes, work values, and expectations of you have influenced your career decision making:

_____

_____

_____

_____

_____

OCCUPATIONAL STEREOTYPING

Briefly summarize how your occupational stereotypes have hindered or helped you in your career decision making:

_____

_____

_____

_____

_____

_____

In this chapter you examined the personal characteristics that make you a unique individual. You explored your personality traits, interests, work values, and aptitudes to give you ideas about what you are like, what you are good at, and what is important to you. In addition, you examined how environmental influences such as socioeconomic status and family background might influence your career development. You also considered how occupational stereotyping can affect the type of occupation you select. Finally, Individual Career Plans #1 and #2 helped you to pull together information about all of the above topics.

EXPLORATION When Jed reflected on how he answered the questions in Chapter Two, he was surprised at how much he really knew about his interests and abilities. Two areas of the self-assessment activities that offered new insights were in identifying his work values and in evaluating the influence his family has on the occupational choices he is considering. Although he had seriously considered joining the family business, his Individual Career Plan revealed a strong interest in the career areas of Humanitarian and Physical Performing.

A career in teaching, coaching, or fitness had interested him, but he was afraid the economic rewards would not be great enough to satisfy him. His work values profile reinforced these ideas, as, in Exercise 2.4b, he had selected independence, interaction, and social as his three most important work values. Jed is now anxious to identify some alternative majors and occupational fields that might match his profile.

Working beside a computer programmer two hours a day, Maria has become increasingly interested in repairing existing computer programs. She likes the problem-solving opportunities involved, as well as the logic and detail needed for this type of work. Maria now is attending the career course class and is excited about attending college. She was not surprised to find that her *Individual Career Plan* reflected her interest in Scientific (solving problems) and in Business Detail (detail work). She discussed her work values (independence, creativity, scientific, and accuracy) with her course instructor, and he reinforced her belief that she could be successful in college.

Summary Checklist   CHAPTER 2

What I have learned

_____ I realize that knowing my strengths and limitations is critical in the career-planning process.

_____ I have determined the relationship between (1) my personality, interests, aptitudes, skills, and values and (2) the careers areas, defined by the U.S. Department of Labor.

_____ I have a better understanding of how my family background and other environmental factors have influenced my attitudes and knowledge about work.

How I can use it

By seeing how the personal information I have brought together in this chapter relates to specific career areas identified by the U.S. Department of Labor, I have systematically identified viable occupational possibilities for myself.

What Do I Need to Know About Occupational Alternatives?

Occupational Information

Gathering and using accurate occupational information is essential if you are to select options that fit your interests, values, aptitudes, and skills. Occupational information can help you to

- narrow or reduce the number of occupations you are considering
- correct stereotypes or inaccurate information you may hold about specific occupations
- generate occupational options you may not have considered
- motivate you to engage in serious career decision making by introducing you to some of the rewards associated with specific occupations

To help you explore, evaluate, and utilize occupational information in your career decision-making process, this chapter covers (1) sources of occupational information and how to evaluate them, (2) work skills, (3) the workforce, and (4) work sites. These will be described in terms of current information and future projections.

The amount and type of occupational information you need depends upon your background. If you have little or no work experience, you probably will want to learn about many occupations. If you have held several jobs, you may want specific information about one specific job, including duties, salary and benefit levels, and the required education and training for that job.

The quality of occupational information currently available varies. The most helpful sources provide a variety of facts about occupations such as

1. the nature of the work performed in that occupation
2. education and training requirements for entry and advancement
3. outlook for employment
4. earnings and benefits
5. personal qualifications, skills, and aptitudes required
6. working conditions
7. related occupations within that field

Sources of Occupational Information

The major sources of occupational information are printed materials, computerized information systems, the Internet, audiovisual materials, informational interviews with workers, and on-the-job or direct experiences. Let's review each of these sources and how they can be useful to you. Think about how you learn best—by reading about occupations, through printed materials or the Internet, by observing and interviewing others, or by trying out an occupation as an intern or a volunteer.

Printed Material

Despite the explosion of computerized information, printed material is still a frequently used source of occupational information. One of the best publications is the *Occupational Outlook Handbook (OOH),* which is available from the U. S. Department of Labor (USDL) and revised roughly every two years. The *OOH* contains information on 35 industries and approximately 850 occupations. The information about each occupation includes job duties, education and training requirements, earnings, working conditions, places of employment, employment trends, and sources of additional information. The occupations are organized into 13 clusters of related jobs. You will use this resource in Exercise 3.1.

The *Dictionary of Occupational Titles (DOT),* also published by the USDL, is a good source of information for occupations not included in the *OOH.* The *DOT* is now available online as O*Net (see next page). Each of the 20,000 occupational definitions included in the printed *DOT* is designated by a nine-digit number. The first of the nine digits refers to one of the nine occupational categories listed below:

1. Professional, technical, and managerial occupations
2. Clerical and sales occupations
3. Service occupations
4. Agricultural, fishery, forestry, and related occupations
5. Processing occupations
6. Machine trades occupations
7. Benchwork occupations
8. Structural work occupations
9. Miscellaneous occupations

These nine occupational categories are further subdivided into occupational areas, and then into occupational groups.

The *Guide for Occupational Exploration (GOE),* a third USDL publication, is another source of occupational information organized around the 12 interest areas you learned about in Chapter Two, 66 work groups, and 348 subgroups. Occupations in the

66 work groups are classified according to the worker's abilities and adaptabilities. *Abilities* include factors such as general educational development, physical capabilities, aptitudes, and job knowledge. *Adaptabilities* refer to adjustments to work situations, including environment, routine, dealing with people, and working to set standards.

Other print resources include *Chronicle Guidance's Occupational Briefs* and the three-volume *Encyclopedia of Careers and Vocational Guidance.* Libraries and career resource centers keep career books and pamphlets both on the shelves and in file drawers. Some libraries even have special areas for career materials. The *Occupational Outlook Quarterly,* an up-to-date occupational magazine, is also available at most libraries and career resource centers.

Computerized Information Systems

Computer systems became increasingly available in the 1990s. Two popular systems are DISCOVER and SIGI PLUS. DISCOVER, available through the American College Testing Program (ACT), includes modules on learning about work, about yourself, and about occupations, as well as educational choices, planning next steps and a career, and making transitions. Users also can access information about two- and four-year colleges, technical and specialized schools, apprenticeship programs, military programs, and graduate/professional schools.

The System of Interactive Guidance and Information, SIGI PLUS, was developed by the Educational Testing Service (ETS). SIGI PLUS proposes that values identification and clarification are basic to an effective career decision-making process. SIGI PLUS includes modules on self-assessment, search strategies, information, skills, preparing, coping, deciding, and next steps (planning). One module, TRANSITIONS, can be particularly helpful to older adults. College career centers may house these and other computerized sources of occupational information, or they may be available in your college library. Check with your instructor or career counselor regarding the availability of such resources.

The Internet

The availability of occupational information on the Internet has increased dramatically. Access to occupational data, as well as other career-related information such as interest inventories, is within the grasp of anyone who owns a personal computer and has an Internet connection or lives close to a public library or a college or university library. Following is a brief introduction to three important occupational databases:

Occupational Outlook Handbook

(http://stats.bls.gov:80/ocohome.htm)

This website contains the full content of the *Occupational Outlook Handbook (OOH)* as published by the U. S. Bureau of Labor Statistics. You can access this site free and browse by occupational category or search using keywords. The *OOH* includes information on more than 200 of the most popular occupations. This site also includes employment projections and articles on topics such as evaluating a job offer.

O*Net

(www.doleta.gov/programs/onet/onet-hp.htm)

The increasing need for up-to-date occupational information has resulted in a web-based version of the *Dictionary of Occupational Titles,* an occupational classification system the U. S. Government has used for more than 40 years. O*Net's database was designed to help people find jobs and help businesses find employees. It will be used in one-stop career centers established through government funds in major cities across the United States. O*Net will be a vital source of information in the future because it can be updated on a regular basis.

Find Your Career: US News

(www4.usnews.com/usnews/edu/beyond/bccguide.htm)

The US News site is one of the more extensive career guides on the Web. It offers expert advice on occupations in the greatest demand now and in the future and links to other important sources of information. This database is searched by occupational categories combined with educational requirements.

Audiovisual Material

Until recently, audiovisual material has been limited to films and filmstrips. Now these have been replaced by audiotapes and videotapes about occupations. Interactive videos, which are similar to some computer programs and in addition include scenes depicting workers in various occupations, are available. For instance, you can observe individuals performing their on-the-job tasks, which will give you more accurate and realistic data than can printed materials. Check your college or university library, career development office, or counseling center for these resources.

Informational Interviews

Interviews with workers in the field can be one of the most stimulating ways for you to collect occupational information. When you talk with individuals at their workplaces, you can ask for information not available by other means. You also can get the "feel" of the work environment to help you decide if the occupation fits your personality and goals.

Before you conduct an informational interview, think of some questions you want to ask. Write down the questions so you are well-prepared. Don't waste the time of the person who has been gracious enough to consent to the interview. In Exercise 3.2 you will be asked to conduct an informational interview, for which sample questions are provided. Informational interviews will be discussed further in Chapter Eight.

The primary advantage of informational interviews is the firsthand knowledge you will gain about the work environment and the work tasks. When you talk with workers about their occupations, however, recognize that their information may be biased. Evaluate the information carefully and, if possible, verify it by consulting other sources.

Direct Experience

Job shadowing, internships, and volunteer work are other ways of gaining direct information about occupations. Job shadowing involves following a worker around for a time—usually a day or two per week. Colleges and universities often help students explore occupations by arranging opportunities for volunteer work or internships. These direct experiences allow individuals to perform actual work responsibilities related to the occupation, thereby giving them a realistic perspective of what it would be like to "do the job."

Even though these experiences take time, they are usually worth the investment, particularly for individuals who have not worked extensively. Contact your advisor or career-planning office to see what local resources are available. If your college does not have a formal process for contacting local workers, use the yellow pages to locate professionals. Many professionals are willing to work with you to establish internships or provide opportunities for you to volunteer your services. We discuss other ways to gather direct information from workers in the discussion on job searches in Chapter Eight.

Evaluating Occupational Information

When you evaluate the career information you gather, always consider possible biases. Robert Hoppock (1976), a career information expert, suggests asking questions that elicit when, where, who, why, and how answers. Keep these questions in mind when you read printed materials, view audiovisuals, or interview workers. Sample questions are:

1. *When* was the information written or prepared? Is it current or out-of-date? In today's world, three years old is probably "out-of-date."
2. *Where* does the information apply—in a city, state, or the entire country?
3. *Who* wrote it? Are the authors reputable?
4. *Why* was it written? Do the authors provide accurate, objective information or are they trying to "sell" you something?
5. *How* was the information collected? Does it appear that the information comes from reliable sources (e.g., statistics on employment trends gathered from state employment agencies or from the U. S. Department of Labor)?

After you have gathered occupational information using one or more of the ways covered in this chapter, you may wish to discuss it with a professor, advisor, parent, spouse, or friend. It is easy to misinterpret information or form an unrealistic picture of an occupation. By talking with someone about both the negative and the positive aspects of the information you have gathered, you are forced to sort fact from fiction.

Future Work Trends

Vast changes have occurred in the workplace. We will examine some of those changes and speculate about what lies ahead.

Many workplaces are in transition. Many organizations downsized their workforces in the 1990s. Among the hardest-hit were AT&T (123,000 jobs), Eastman Kodak (16,800 jobs), and Delta Airlines (18,800 jobs). On the other hand, at the turn of the millennium we were living in what was being called the tightest U. S. labor market in three decades (*Newsweek,* February 1, 1999). In contrast to downsizing, the 1990s also saw an unbelievable growth in jobs. The "jobs boom" helped to create confidence among young workers who encountered work opportunities never seen by their parents.

The mixed messages that come from downsizing and hypergrowth in jobs can create anxiety among workers and can account, in part, for the tendency of today's workers to express less loyalty to their current employers and be ready to change jobs when presented with other enticing opportunities.

Many claim that the United States is in the middle of a revolution that is having as much impact on work as the Industrial Revolution did in the 19th century. By the beginning of the 21st century, several trends were evident:

- Workers will not stay in one job or work in one organization for the majority of their work lives.
- With competition growing in a global economy, the speed and quality of responses to customer needs dictate what companies remain in business.

- Just-in-time production reduces the workforce to a core of workers with the need for greater contract workers.
- Skilled workers are needed for high-performance workplaces.
- Skilled workers have opportunities in other companies and organizations if their current employers do not meet their needs.

Work Skills Needed in the Next Decade

What skills are needed in today's changing workplace? What skills do the workers of today and tomorrow really need? Meister (1994) suggests these six core workplace competencies as ones that employers see as necessary.

1. *Learning skills:* Workers must learn from several different sources including co-workers, customers and clients, and educational institutions. Their goals must include a commitment to ongoing improvement of their work skills.
2. *Basic reading, writing, computation, and cognitive reasoning skills:* Employees not only must possess the basic skills but also have to be able to apply these skills to work situations.
3. *Interpersonal skills:* Because working in teams is so important in today's and tomorrow's workplace, well-developed interpersonal skills, including conflict resolution skills, are necessary to succeed.
4. *Creative thinking and problem-solving skills:* Problem-solving requires the ability to analyze situations, ask questions, and think in innovative ways to generate options.
5. *Leadership and visioning skills:* Cutting-edge workers are those who are able to see opportunities for improvement in their work settings and are not afraid to suggest ways in which the organization can change and grow.
6. *Self-development and self-management skills:* Workers will need to take charge of their own careers and, in fact, manage their own development. They will be expected to keep improving their skills for current assignments and take responsibility for developing new skills.

Robert Barner (1994) suggests that you become a career strategist, not just a career planner. He writes about the need to take the initiative to chart your own career direction. Rather than look for "job security," you should be seeking "job resiliency"—which means that you are able to shift with ease to the requirements of a new or changing job. Acquiring the skills to make these shifts is crucial if you are to adapt competently to new work situations.

Barner describes four key survival skills:

- *Environmental scanning:* the need to prevent your technological obsolescence by tapping into computer and personal networks to continually update your skills. Staying current in your field is critical to this process. Once you have determined the market value of your skills, you can identify potential employers and take advantage of new employment opportunities.
- *Portable skills:* skills that can be transferred to many work settings. Examples are knowledge of standard business software and project management. These skills can help you cross organizational lines.
- *Self-management:* the ability to work effectively alone or as a member of a work team.
- *Communication skills:* includes both verbal and written communication tools. The settings in which communicating is especially important include high-stress, time-limited, and culturally diverse situations. Also key is the ability to communicate clearly and concisely over the Internet and other electronic devices.

Many of these skills are integral to coursework and other in- and out-of-class experiences that you can learn during your college years. In Chapter Two you identified the skills you presently possess. You may want to return to that chapter to determine which of the skills listed here are ones that you need to improve or acquire.

Workforce Trends in the Next Decade

Making informed career decisions requires reliable information about opportunities for the future. As you begin to make specific occupational choices, you will need to stay current about general workforce trends as well as the demand for specific occupations. Understanding the changing nature of the workforce and the supply and demand for particular occupations will help you choose a career with a future. This section examines some thought-provoking trends and projections for the next decade.

Population

Population is the single most important factor in determining the size and composition of the labor force. Changes in population influence the demand for goods and services and thereby affect employment opportunities. For instance, a growing and aging population has resulted in an increased demand for health services. Population changes also produce corresponding changes in the size and demographic composition of the labor force. By 2008, the U. S. population is expected to increase by 23 million. This is roughly the same rate of growth as during the 1988–98 period but significantly slower than over the 1978–88 period (see Figure 3.1).

Growth in population and labor force, 1978–88, 1988–98, and projected 1998–2008.   **FIGURE 3.1**

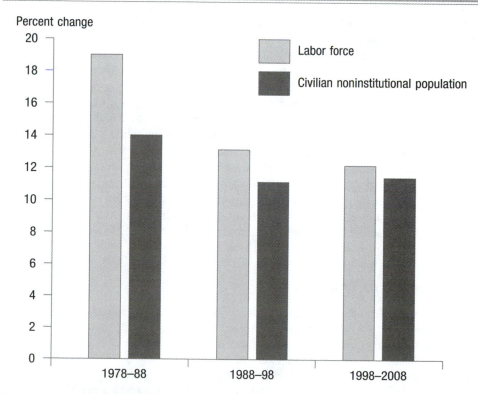

Source: *Occupational Outlook Handbook,* 2000–2001.

FIGURE 3.2 *Percent of labor force by race and ethnic origin, 1998 and projected 2008.*

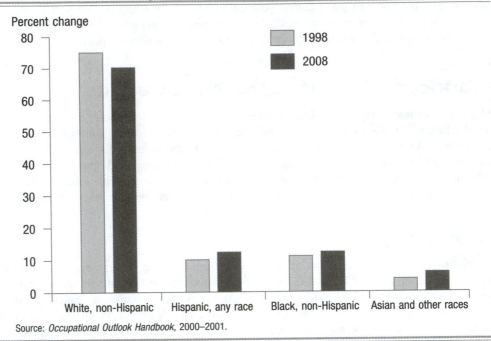

Source: *Occupational Outlook Handbook,* 2000–2001.

SIZE. The labor force is defined as people who are either working or looking for work. The civilian labor force is expected to increase by 17 million, or 12 percent, to 154.6 million by 2008.

COMPOSITION. The U.S. workforce will become more diverse by 2008. White, non-Hispanic persons will make up a decreasing share of the labor force, from 73.9 to 70.7 percent. Hispanics, non-Hispanic blacks, Asians, and other racial groups are projected to make up an increasing share of the labor force by 2008 (Figure 3.2). Hispanics will increase from 10.4 to 12.7 percent; non-Hispanic blacks from 11.6 to 12.4 percent; and Asians from 4.6 percent to 5.7 percent.

The number of men and women in the labor force will grow, but the number of men will grow at a slower rate than in the past. By 2008, men's share of the labor force is expected to decrease from 53.7 to 52.5 percent while women's share is expected to increase from 46.3 to 47.5 percent.

The youth population, ages 16 to 24, is expected to increase as a share of the population to 16 percent. This is the first increase in this age group since the 1970s. The group of workers 25–44 years old, who comprised 52 percent of the labor force in 1998, is expected to decline to 44 percent of the labor force by 2008. Workers 45 and older, on the other hand, are projected to increase from 33 to 40 percent of the labor force during the same time period (see Figure 3.3).

Education and Training

Expected job growth varies widely by education and training requirements. Five of the six education and training categories projected to have the highest percent change require that workers have at least a bachelor's degree (see Figure 3.4). These five categories will account for one-third of all employment growth to 2008. While employment in occupations that do not require postsecondary education are projected to grow by about 12 percent, those occupations that require a bachelor's degree will grow by almost 22 percent. Education is becoming absolutely crucial in obtaining a high-paying job. All but a few of the 50 highest paying occupations require a college degree.

Percent of labor force by age group, 1998 and projected 2008.   **FIGURE 3.3**

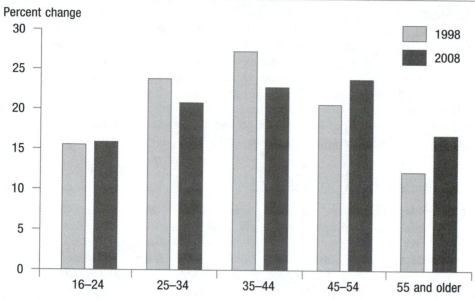

Source: *Occupational Outlook Handbook*, 2000–2001.

Growth rates by most significant source of education and training, projected 1998–2008.   **FIGURE 3.4**

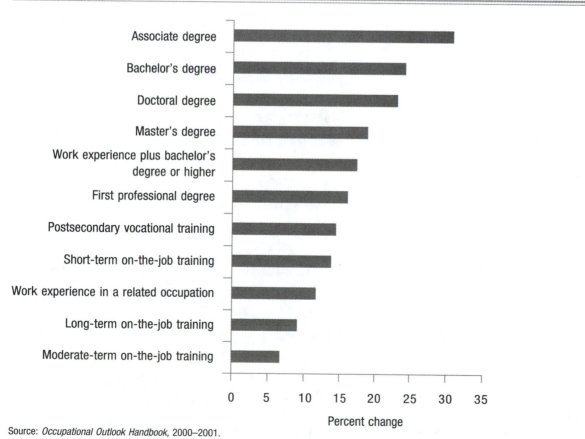

Source: *Occupational Outlook Handbook*, 2000–2001.

Worksites in the Next Decade

Total employment is expected to increase 14 percent, from 141 million in 1998 to 161 million in 2008. The 20 million jobs added by 2008 will not be distributed equally across the major industrial and occupational groups. The long-term shift from goods-producing to service-producing employment is expected to continue (see Figures 3.5 and 3.6). Service-producing industries include (1) services; (2) transportation and public utilities; (3) finance, insurance, and real estate; (4) wholesale and retail trade; and (5) government. These jobs are expected to account for approximately 19.1 million of the 19.5 new wage and salary jobs generated through 2008. A brief description of growth in each area follows.

Service-Producing Industries

SERVICES. The largest and fastest growing major industry group, services, is expected to add 11.8 million new jobs by 2008. Almost three-fourths of this projected job growth is concentrated in three sectors of services: business, health, and professional and miscellaneous services. Business services, including personnel supply and computer and data-processing services, will add 4.6 million jobs. Health services, including home health care services, nursing, and personal care facilities, will add 2.8 million jobs. Professional and miscellaneous services, including management, public relations, and research and testing services, will add 1.1 million jobs.

FIGURE 3.5 *Percent change in wage and salary employment, service-producing industries, 1988–98 and projected 1998–2008.*

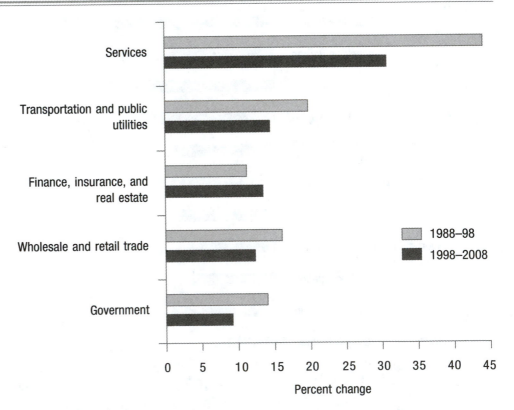

Source: *Occupational Outlook Handbook,* 2000–2001.

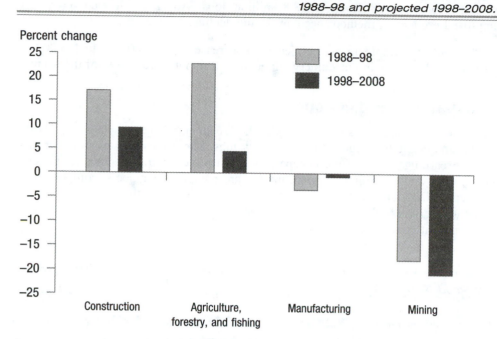

Percent change in wage and salary employment, goods-producing industries, 1988–98 and projected 1998–2008.   **FIGURE 3.6**

Source: *Occupational Outlook Handbook*, 2000–2001.

TRANSPORTATION AND PUBLIC UTILITIES.   Employment in this sector will increase by 14 percent, or 674,000 jobs. Employment in the transportation sector is expected to increase by 16 percent, and employment in communications is expected to add 300,000 new jobs by 2008. On the other hand, employment in utilities is expected to decline by roughly 4 percent.

FINANCE, INSURANCE, AND REAL ESTATE.   Employment is expected to increase by 13 percent, adding 960,000 jobs and reaching a total of 7.4 million. The demand for financial services is expected to continue, as is the demand in the security and commodity brokers sector of the industry.

WHOLESALE AND RETAIL TRADE.   Employment is expected to increase by 7 and 14 percent, respectively, growing from 6.8 million to 7.3 million in wholesale trade and from 22.3 to 25.4 million in retail trade.

GOVERNMENT.   By 2008, government employment, including public education and public hospitals, is expected to increase by more than 9 percent, from 19.8 to 21.7 million jobs. Education will drive employment growth in this area.

Goods-Producing Industries

Employment in the goods-producing industries has been relatively stagnant since the early 1980s. This sector is expected to grow by 1.6 percent over the next decade.

CONSTRUCTION.   Construction is expected to increase by 9 percent, from 5.9 to 6.5 million jobs. The demand for new housing and construction of roads, bridges, and tunnels will account for the growth in this area.

AGRICULTURE, FORESTRY, AND FISHING.   Overall employment in agriculture, forestry, and fishing is expected to increase by nearly 5 percent, from 2.2 to 2.3 million.

MANUFACTURING. Manufacturing employment is projected to decline by less than 1 percent from a 1998 level of 18.8 million jobs. Advances in technology and improved production methods account for the decline.

MINING. Mining employment is projected to decrease by 590,000 jobs to 475,000, or 19 percent. Labor-saving machinery and increased imports are causes of the decline.

Occupational Projections

The 20 occupational areas listed in Figure 3.7 are among those projected to grow the fastest and create the largest number of new jobs. These jobs also have higher than average earnings. Half of the occupations are involved with computer technology, health care, and education. Topping the list are computer engineers, computer support specialists, and computer systems analysts, reflecting the high demand for computer services. You may want to revisit your Individual Career Plan (Chapter Two) in light of this information.

FIGURE 3.7 *Occupations with fast growth and high pay that have the largest numerical growth, projected 1998–2008.*

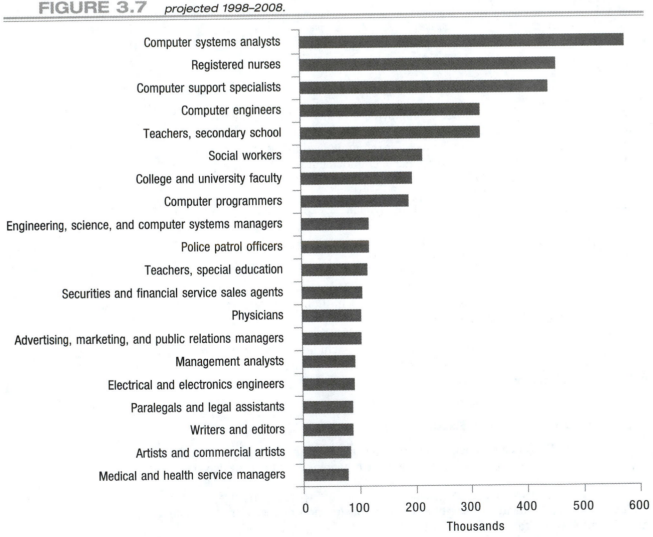

Source: *Occupational Outlook Handbook,* 2000–2001.

In addition to the U.S. government, many sources have made predictions about work in the future. For example, *Time* magazine (May 22, 2000), forecasts that the 10 hottest jobs in the upcoming decade will include tissue engineers (artificial skin is already on the market, and other artificial tissue soon will be available) and "pharmers" (new-age farmers who will raise crops and livestock that have been genetically engineered to produce therapeutic proteins).

Now that you have learned about the importance of occupational information and have reviewed labor force and labor market information, you will want to do some searching on your own. Exercise 3.1 will take you on a web-based exploration of the occupations that interest you, and in Exercise 3.2 you will conduct an informational interview.

Exploring Occupational Information EXERCISE 3.1

To get the most out of this exercise, you need access to the Internet. If you do not own a computer, ask your instructor where you can locate a computer on campus. Examine the list of occupations which are representative of the Career Interest Areas you identified when you completed Individual Career Plan #1 in Chapter Two. Then name two occupations about which you want to learn more:

_____ and _____

Now access *the Occupational Outlook Handbook (OOH)* on the Internet at this address:

http://stats.bls.gov/ocohome.htm

Once you have found the *OOH* on the web, you can learn more about specific occupations simply by entering the name of the occupation in the "Search by Occupation" box. Search for information about the two occupations in which you are most interested, and answer the following questions about each one:

Occupational Search Questions #1

1. Name of occupation: _____

2. What are the major work responsibilities of this occupation?

_____

_____

3. What skills are needed to enter this occupation?

_____

_____

4. What education and training are needed for the occupation?

_____

_____

5. What are the working conditions of the occupation (e.g., hours, work environment, dress requirements, hazards, travel, type of supervision)?

_____

_____

Typical Occupations in the Career Interest Areas

CAREER INTEREST AREAS	SAMPLE OCCUPATIONS
01 Artistic	writer, poet, editor, critic, painter, designer, photographer, art teacher, art director, makeup artist, decorator, jeweler, sign painter, announcer, actor, director, singer, musician, music arranger, dancer, choreographer, photographer's model, dress-designer model
02 Scientific	astronomer, chemist, geologist, mathematician, environmental analyst, materials scientist, flight surgeon, dentist, veterinary livestock inspector, veterinarian, audiologist, sample tester, hot-cell technician, pharmacist, biological aide, embalmer, computer programmer, computer scientist
03 Plants and Animals	farmer, fisherman, forester, wildlife control agent, park worker supervisor, animal trainer, animal caretaker, rancher, plant nursery worker
04 Protective	correction officer, jailer, firefighter, police detective, patrol officer, sheriff, fire marshall, park superintendent
05 Mechanical	aerodynamicist, health physicist, power system electrical engineer, research mechanic, air traffic controller, building inspector, navigator, flight control manager, airplane pilot, water treatment plant operator, locomotive engineer, tow truck operator, machine driller, bulldozer operator, bricklayer, carpenter, electrician, construction worker, pharmacy helper
06 Industrial	machine operator, assembler, press operator, machine tester, mill supervisor, buzzsaw operator, drill punch operator, weigher, grader
07 Business Detail	bookkeeper, account analyst, payroll clerk, ticket agent, cashier, teller, toll collector, computer operator, file clerk, process server, real estate clerk, claims clerk, travel clerk, credit clerk, traffic clerk, mail carrier, mortgage closing clerk
08 Selling (Persuasive)	estate planner, public utilities sales representative, grain buyer, automobile salesperson, auctioneer, real estate agent
09 Accommodating	sightseeing guide, hunting guide, hostess, flight attendant, hairstylist, barber, bus driver, driving instructor, automobile rental clerk, caddie, conductor
10 Humanitarian	minister, parole officer, counselor, dental hygienist, medical technologist, respiratory therapist, primary-grades teacher, nurse, emergency medical technician, athletic trainer, social worker
11 Social/Business	newswriter, columnist/commentator, interpreter, fashion coordinator, lobbyist, airport manager, purchasing agent, engineering analyst, applied statistician, underwriter, trust officer, secondary school teacher, librarian, developmental psychologist, sociologist, anthropologist, job analyst, economist, hospital administrator, academic dean
12 Physical	professional sports scout, head coach, umpire, race car driver, professional athlete, rodeo performer, stunt performer, assistant coach

6. What earnings and benefits are associated with the occupation?

_____

_____

7. What are the projected employment opportunities in the occupation?

_____

_____

Occupational Search Questions #2

1. Name of occupation: _____

2. What are the major work responsibilities of this occupation?

_____

_____

3. What skills are needed to enter this occupation?

_____

_____

4. What education and training are needed for the occupation?

_____

_____

5. What are the working conditions of the occupation (e.g., hours, work environment, dress requirements, hazards, travel, type of supervision)?

_____

_____

6. What earnings and benefits are associated with the occupation?

_____

_____

7. What are the projected employment opportunities in the occupation?

_____

_____

What is your reaction to the information you learned from the *Occupational Outlook Handbook?*

_____

_____

_____

_____

Did any of the information you discovered surprise you or increase or decrease your interest in the occupation?

_____

Now that you have learned more about each of your occupational choices, you will benefit from talking with someone who is actually working in that occupation. In Exercise 3.2 you will learn how to conduct an informational interview.

EXERCISE 3.2   *Informational Interview*

The informational interview is another important way to learn about occupations. Consult your university or college advisor for help in arranging an interview with someone who works in one of the occupations you searched on the Internet. Sample interview questions are presented below. Photocopy the questions to use during your interview, and add questions of your own if you wish.

Name of Occupation: _____

1. What led to your choice of this occupation?

2. What skills do you need for this work?

3. What are your major work responsibilities?

4. What is a typical day like in your work?

5. How did you prepare for your job?

6. If you were hiring a person for your job, what qualifications would you look for?

7. What are the working conditions on your job (e.g., hours, work environment, dress requirements, hazards, travel, type of supervision)?

_____

_____

_____

8. What is the employment outlook for your occupation?

_____

_____

_____

9. What is the entry-level pay for this occupation?

_____

_____

_____

10. What other occupations are closely related to this one?

_____

_____

_____

11. What advice would you give to someone who is thinking about pursuing this occupation?

_____

_____

_____

Reflection Points

1. What was the most important information you gained from the interview?

_____

_____

_____

2. How does this information fit with what you already know?

_____

_____

_____

3. What did you learn that might prove useful in your career search?

_____

_____

_____

At this point, you should be ready to identify some tentative occupational choices. You have examined your personality traits, interests, values, aptitudes, and skills. You have read about occupations that are compatible with your interests and values, and you may have tried to conduct an informational interview. Now list the occupations that most appeal to you.

1. _____

2. _____

3. _____

Jed and Maria

EXPLORATION Jed had thought only vaguely about what employment opportunities would be available when he would graduate, but he realized that he needed to take this information into account in his career planning. As an assignment for his class, he visited the career planning office on his campus. He was amazed at all the resources available to explore occupational information—printed information and computerized career information systems including the Internet.

Jed decided to gather in-depth information about the field of fitness. He was surprised by all the occupations, in addition to teaching and coaching, associated with fitness. On the Internet he found information about exercise science; sports psychology; recreation, physical, and occupational therapies; and athletic trainer. He also was surprised to learn about the salaries in some of these areas, as they were higher than he expected. He decided to explore these possibilities further with his career course instructor and his academic advisor.

Maria wanted to find more specific information about opportunities as a computer programmer, so she accessed the *Occupational Outlook Handbook (OOH)* on the Web (http://stats.bls.gov:80/ocohome.htm). This website included employment projections and articles on various career-related topics. The *OOH* had a long section on the nature of the work that computer programmers do.

As Maria read about the work tasks, she was surprised to find how many she readily understood because of what she had learned in her current job. This search helped her realize that she had acquired more knowledge and skills in the field than she thought. Potential earnings in the field were more than double her current pay, and she also discovered that computer programming is one of the occupations expected to be in demand during the next decade. In fact, employment opportunities in the field looked excellent.

This chapter has explored the value of occupational information and described its major sources: printed materials, computerized information systems, audiovisual materials, occupational interviews, and direct experiences. In addition, you examined supply-and-demand projections and learned how to use the *Occupational Outlook Handbook,* an important resource. Using the *OOH,* you narrowed down your career alternatives. Your next step is to integrate the occupational information you have compiled with the necessary education and training.

Summary Checklist   CHAPTER 3

What I have learned

_____ I know where to locate occupational information and have used a variety of sources to explore some specific occupations.

_____ I have considered how workforce trends and projections may affect me in the future and have included this information in my career exploration.

_____ I have talked with workers in the field(s) I am seriously considering at this point and have included this information in my planning.

How I can use it

I now have solid occupational information upon which to base a decision. If I need to reconsider my choice or when I need to make a new work-related decision in the future, I will know what information resources work best for me, how to find them, and how to apply the information to my new situation.

What Do I Need to Know About Educational Alternatives?

Choosing an Educational Direction

As you formulate more definitive occupational plans, your choices about your education become an important consideration. Whether you are a first-year college student, a sophomore, or an older adult pondering a career change, selecting the appropriate type and level of education is a multifaceted decision. Your career aspirations often suggest or even dictate the type and level of educational preparation you need to enter the workforce. For example, if you wish to become a social worker aide, you will want to attend a two-year technical college that will give you direct occupational training for that work. If you wish to be a social worker, you will need a baccalaureate degree. If you wish to be a social agency administrator, you would do best to obtain a graduate degree (e.g., a master's in social work [MSW], a master's in counseling [MA], or a master's in public administration [MPA]).

The U. S. Department of Labor describes several educational programs that provide the knowledge and skills required at different levels of occupations:

Graduate   Occupations such as business manager or college professor often require graduate studies involving one or more years of schooling beyond the baccalaureate degree. Examples of graduate degrees are an MBA (master's in business administration), an MFA (master's of fine arts), or a Ph.D. (doctoral degree).

College   Some occupations—for example, museum curator and medical technologist—require undergraduate studies that lead to a baccalaureate degree—bachelor of arts (BA) or bachelor of science (BS).

Technical	Technical programs beyond the high school level prepare the student for specific occupations or teach skills needed for a particular type of work. Earning a technical degree usually takes from six months to two years and often leads to a two-year associate's degree (AA) or a certificate (e.g., an AA in engineering technology or a professional nanny certificate). This type of preparation is offered at technical schools, community colleges, and some four-year colleges and universities.
Vocational	High school level vocational programs fall into this category. These programs focus on specific occupations or skills. Examples include automotive technology and business education.

You also may acquire education or training through apprenticeships, military service, or other specialized programs. A few occupations, such as cashier and clerk, require no formal training or education other than a general or high school diploma, but on-the-job experience is required for some jobs in the trades.

Some occupations require credentials such as licenses, certificates, degrees, or diplomas. To work in professional occupations (e.g., health, architecture, education), you probably will need to follow a highly structured educational program specifically designed to prepare students for state and/or national licensing or certification tests. Formal education and training are fast becoming prerequisites for jobs in today's work world.

Although the information in this chapter focuses primarily on a college education, it is important to become familiar with other educational options as well. Some students select a two-year college but later transfer to a four-year program. Other students enroll in a four-year college and discover that a two-year technical degree would be better suited to their interests, abilities, and career goals. Keep in mind that any decision you make now is not necessarily permanent. You may wish to change careers at any age, and a new career may require a different type of education or training. In Exercise 4.1 you will answer the question of what type of education you need.

EXERCISE 4.1   *What Type of Education Do I Need?*

What education do you want to complete (for example, four-year college degree, technical degree, graduate degree)?

_____

_____

_____

Do you need other information to confirm this choice? If so, where will you obtain it (for example, college admissions office, college catalogues, professional organizations, academic advisors, college faculty)?

_____

_____

_____

How does this type of education fit with your future goals? For example, will you need a four-year degree in business to obtain a job in the field you are considering?

_____

_____

_____

Why Attend College?

People attend college for many reasons. Some consider it preparation for a job. Others value a college degree for the broad education it provides. They enjoy learning for learning's sake. Still others consider it a personal accomplishment. Our value system often determines the reasons we enroll in higher education. In Exercise 4.2 you will consider why you are in college.

Why Am I in College?   EXERCISE 4.2

Following are some academic, personal, and career reasons for attending college. Read them all and then check the five that are most important to you.

_____ To learn for the sake of learning

_____ To become proficient in reading and study skills

_____ To improve my ability to think and reason

_____ To broaden my intellectual interests

_____ To choose an area of study that will be interesting and challenging to me

_____ To enjoy a variety of cultural activities

_____ To learn how to become an effective leader

_____ To make my family proud of me

_____ To make lifelong friends

_____ To participate in the social opportunities on campus

_____ To take courses that lead directly to an occupational field

_____ To learn the skills necessary to find a good job when I graduate

_____ To prepare myself for a certain lifestyle

_____ To help me make more money in my work

_____ To prepare for graduate school

Are the five reasons you checked above mainly academic, personal, or career-related? What does this tell you?

_____

_____

How do these reasons affect your life as a student? How will they affect you after graduation?

_____

_____

Making Initial Decisions

Charlie decided in high school to become an engineer. His teachers encouraged him to use his math and science abilities in a career. Charlie's father and sister are professional engineers, so he had experience working in an engineering firm during the summers. Charlie declared an engineering major when he entered college. Although he is not sure what branch of engineering he wants to pursue, he is certain he has made the right choice.

Some students like Charlie enter college with specific career aspirations. They are aware of their abilities and interests and, through their research and experience, understand exactly what is expected in a particular work environment. These students have put careful thought into their decisions, often based on solid information and experiences. If you were as "decided" as Charlie, you might not be reading this book.

Though most students have several possible majors in mind, they may not be ready to make a choice.

Carla had many interests when she entered college but was not ready to declare a major. She chose to be "undecided" and entered a special advising program for students who are unsure of their major. Carla's strengths are in language, art, and the social sciences. She can test her ideas before deciding on a major by taking a variety of courses in these areas. Her academic advisor is helping her sort through her options. Carla also has visited the college's career center, where she is gathering information about herself and possible majors and careers.

It is common for students to be undecided during the first year of college. At some point, though, they will need to spend time purposefully exploring possible careers. Some campuses have excellent resources to assist students with this exploration. Most colleges and universities have a career planning center that offers career counseling, testing, a career library, and computerized career information systems. Students who are not sure about their direction need to take responsibility for actively researching various occupational options. The skills they use in doing this will prove useful as they make decisions throughout their college years and beyond.

Sam entered college and declared a business major. He was not certain that he wanted to be a businessman at the time, but he chose that area because he wanted a well-paying job after college. Sam was bored and did not do well in several of his core business classes. He did do well, however, in his English and social science courses. By the middle of his sophomore year, he knew he wanted to change his major. He worked with his academic advisor, who helped him to identify other majors more closely related to his interests and abilities.

While first-year college students are exploring their options, upper-level students sometimes find that their initial choice of major is not as satisfying as they originally thought and now want to change direction. They discover that they have no interest in or talent for their initial choices. They are in a different situation from that of first-year students, because now they have a record of coursework that may give them insight into their strengths and limitations. Other students, particularly at large universities, find they are closed out of certain majors because of highly selective admissions requirements.

Once Sam recognized his desire to change majors, he sought help. After carefully appraising his strengths and limitations, he selected a public relations major because it fulfilled his interest and talent in writing and his desire to work in a business setting. Unfortunately, some students do not follow Sam's path; they leave school before examining all of their alternatives.

During high school Angie worked part-time answering phones at a hospital and became interested in preparing for a job in a health-related field. She sought an education that would be practical, give her hands-on experience, and prepare her to enter a specific occupation. She enrolled in a local community college program in emergency medical technology. When she completes her training, she will be certified as a paramedic. She now works in the hospital emergency room part-time while going to school. Angie is very excited about her future.

Technical education meets the needs of many students who want to learn specific skills. Earning an associate's degree is an excellent avenue for students who want practical preparation for a challenging and satisfying career.

The Undergraduate Curriculum

One of the biggest differences between a two- and four-year degree is the curriculum. A technical education focuses on acquiring the skills needed to perform certain tasks in a technical occupation. Some two-year associate degrees fulfill the requirements for the first two years of a baccalaureate degree. Four-year degrees, however, usually include a general introduction to many subjects with the intent of providing students a broad base of knowledge in addition to a specialization or major.

Most baccalaureate degree programs have specific course requirements, including courses in the humanities, social sciences, and science. Some majors require students to take certain courses in a related area. For example, a student with an engineering major must take physics classes. Some colleges require students to take courses with an international or a multicultural focus.

Technical programs such as engineering often have basic course requirements that include writing and math components. These basic courses, rather than offering a general approach, focus on specific skills applicable to the pertinent technical area.

Many baccalaureate programs are highly structured and allow students limited opportunities to take elective courses. These programs often lead to a degree with a professional focus, such as physical therapy, architecture, or engineering, and emphasize the skill-building necessary to fulfill the requirements for those professions. Some professional programs not only require a set of core courses but also expect students to acquire a breadth of knowledge in many fields, which will help them to be intellectually well-rounded.

Students often perceive that a liberal arts degree will not prepare them for a job. It is more realistic for them to consider a liberal arts education as preparation for life and a career rather than as "job training." If students have interests in a variety of subjects and want more control over their coursework, their choice of a liberal arts degree can provide the flexibility they desire. Majors in the liberal arts also may prepare students for professional or graduate programs, for example, if their career goals include pre-law, teacher certification, college teaching, or business.

Although a major in history, biology, or English may not lead directly to a specific occupation, it can prepare students for a wide range of career opportunities. Liberal arts students majoring in their favorite subject also must plan carefully for entering the workforce. To gain the broad knowledge and skills that many employers demand, they must consider taking additional courses in writing, communications, human relations, logic, computer science, or languages.

Choosing a Major

When students consider choosing a major, they might invoke the "chicken and egg" question: "Which should I choose first—an occupation, and then determine what majors might lead to that work, or should I choose a major and then figure out what occupations are relevant?" Either approach is legitimate. If you cannot decide on a career field right away but you know what academic subjects interest you, consider making the educational decision first. On the other hand, you might be able to decide on a general career direction, such as business, but you might not be sure of the major that will best lead you where you want to go.

Some students decide on a career field for which a very specific education is required, such as nursing, electrical engineering, or teaching. The educational and occupational decision is the same for them, and they can easily select their majors. A four-year program allows students to question and test their first decision. If they take the general education requirements that provide a base of coursework, they can later choose almost any major.

In a survey by the U. S. Department of Labor, 50 percent of college graduates indicated that their jobs were closely related to their college majors. The figures ranged from 13 percent of history majors to 92 percent in nursing. Only 57 percent of engineering graduates were in closely related jobs; 31 percent said their jobs were somewhat related to their majors.

When you select a major, ask yourself: "Does this major reflect a careful analysis of my academic strengths, limitations, interests, values, experiences, and other characteristics that make me a unique person? Am I aware of the different paths within this general career field?" For example, if you are interested in business, do you picture yourself becoming an entrepreneur, working for a large corporation, working in the public sector, or holding a job in a bank? Exercise 4.3 is designed for you to match your interests to the college majors that apply.

Different majors may prepare students for the same occupational area. Business, journalism, communications, and English majors all offer good preparation for a public relations position. A physics or history major may lead to a public relations job, too, if one's preparation includes courses in writing and marketing. Your related work experiences, leadership qualities, or demonstrated talent in the skills needed for the job you seek may be just as important to an employer as your actual degree or major.

EXERCISE 4.3 Matching My Interests and Abilities with Majors

Using the information you collected in Chapter Two, examine the list of majors in the matrix and match the interest areas and abilities with your own.

1. At the top of the matrix, circle the three Interest Areas you recorded in Exercise 2.3 in Chapter Two.

2. Also circle the three aptitudes you recorded in Exercise 2.5.

3. As you read down each column you circled, stop at each dot and circle it. Do this for all six columns.

4. Reading across, find the college majors with two or more circled dots. (A major with many circled dots indicates a good one to explore, as it probably will be a realistic match for your interests and aptitudes.)

5. Place a checkmark in the left column beside the majors you wish to explore in more depth.

Majors that fit my interests:

_____

_____

Majors that fit my aptitudes:

_____

_____

Majors that fit both my interests and aptitudes:

_____

_____

Are these the same majors you have considered? Did you find new ideas for majors that might interest you? Which ones?

_____

_____

College majors and related interests and aptitudes.

Check here if you wish to explore this major further	COLLEGE MAJOR	INTERESTS (Exercise 2.3) Artistic	Scientific	Nature	Protective (Law Enforcement)	Mechanical/Industrial	Business Detail	Selling (Persuasive)	Humanitarian	Social/Business Mgt.	Physical Performing (Sports)	APTITUDES (Exercise 2.5) Artistic/Creative	Communications/Verbal	Communications/Writing	Math/Computational	Mechanical	Leading/Teaching	Scientific	Social
	Accounting						•						•	•	•				
	Administration, Business						•			•			•	•	•		•		•
	Administration, Education						•			•			•	•	•		•		•
	Advertising	•						•		•			•	•					•
	Aeronautical Engineering		•			•									•			•	
	Agriculture		•	•			•							•	•			•	
	Ag Economics		•				•			•					•			•	
	Ag Engineering		•			•									•				
	Agronomy		•												•			•	
	Animal Science		•	•														•	
	Anthropology		•															•	
	Architecture	•	•									•			•			•	
	Art, General Fine Arts	•										•						•	
	Art Education	•										•					•		
	Astronomy		•												•				
	Biology		•	•											•			•	
	Botany		•	•											•			•	
	Cell Biology		•	•														•	
	Ceramic Engineering		•			•												•	
	Ceramics	•										•						•	
	Chemical Engineering		•			•												•	
	Chemistry		•													•		•	
	Child Development		•							•									•
	Chinese									•			•	•					
	Classics									•			•	•					
	Clothing and Textiles	•	•									•						•	
	Communications							•		•			•	•					•

(continued)

		INTERESTS (Exercise 2.3)										APTITUDES (Exercise 2.5)							
Check here if you wish to explore this major further	COLLEGE MAJOR	Artistic	Scientific	Nature	Protective (Law Enforcement)	Mechanical/Industrial	Business Detail	Selling (Persuasive)	Humanitarian	Social/Business Mgt.	Physical Performing (Sports)	Artistic/Creative	Communications/Verbal	Communications/Writing	Math/Computational	Mechanical	Leading/Teaching	Scientific	Social
	Computer/Info Science		•			•	•								•			•	
	Consumer Economics					•				•			•	•					•
	Criminology				•				•										•
	Dance	•										•							
	Dental Hygiene								•										•
	Dentistry		•						•									•	
	Dietetics		•															•	
	Earth Sciences		•												•			•	
	Economics						•								•				
	Education, Elementary									•									•
	Education, Secondary (depends on subject)									•									•
	Engineering		•			•									•	•		•	
	English								•			•		•					
	Environmental Science		•	•		•									•			•	
	Fashion Merchandising						•	•											•
	Finance						•			•					•				•
	Fine Arts	•										•							
	Food Sciences and Tech		•	•		•												•	
	Foreign Languages									•			•	•					
	Forestry		•	•														•	
	French									•			•	•					
	Genetics		•												•			•	
	Geography		•															•	
	Geology		•												•			•	
	German									•			•	•					
	Health Education																		•
	History									•			•	•					
	Horticulture		•	•			•					•			•			•	

(continued)

Check here if you wish to explore this major further	COLLEGE MAJOR	INTERESTS (Exercise 2.3)										APTITUDES (Exercise 2.5)							
		Artistic	Scientific	Nature	Protective (Law Enforcement)	Mechanical/Industrial	Business Detail	Selling (Persuasive)	Humanitarian	Social/Business Mgt.	Physical Performing (Sports)	Artistic/Creative	Communications/Verbal	Communications/Writing	Math/Computational	Mechanical	Leading/Teaching	Scientific	Social
	Insurance						•	•		•			•	•	•				•
	Interior Design	•										•	•						
	Islamic Studies									•				•					•
	Journalism									•			•	•					•
	Landscape Architecture	•	•	•								•			•			•	
	Library Science									•			•	•					•
	Linguistics									•			•	•					•
	Marketing						•	•		•			•	•					•
	Mathematics						•			•					•				
	Mechanical Engineering		•			•									•	•		•	
	Medicine		•						•				•					•	•
	Microbiology		•															•	
	Music	•										•							
	Natural Resources Management		•	•	•		•								•			•	
	Nursing		•						•				•					•	•
	Nutrition		•															•	
	Occupational Therapy	•	•						•			•					•	•	•
	Oceanography		•	•											•			•	
	Optometry		•						•						•			•	
	Parks and Recreation Management		•					•	•										•
	Pharmacy		•												•			•	
	Philosophy																		•
	Physical Education										•						•		•
	Physical Therapy			•					•						•	•		•	•
	Physics		•												•			•	
	Political Science									•			•	•					•
	Psychology		•						•				•	•				•	•
	Public Relations							•					•	•					•

(continued)

Check here if you wish to explore this major further	COLLEGE MAJOR	INTERESTS (Exercise 2.3)										APTITUDES (Exercise 2.5)							
		Artistic	Scientific	Nature	Protective (Law Enforcement)	Mechanical/Industrial	Business Detail	Selling (Persuasive)	Humanitarian	Social/Business Mgt.	Physical Performing (Sports)	Artistic/Creative	Communications/Verbal	Communications/Writing	Math/Computational	Mechanical	Leading/Teaching	Scientific	Social
	Real Estate						•	•											•
	Recreation								•	•	•		•						•
	Religious Studies								•				•	•					•
	Russian									•			•	•					
	Slavic Studies									•			•	•					
	Social Work								•				•	•					•
	Spanish									•			•	•					
	Special Education								•	•		•					•		•
	Speech and Hearing Therapy								•				•						•
	Statistics				•					•					•				
	Veterinary Medicine		•	•														•	
	Wildlife Management		•	•														•	
	Zoology		•	•														•	

Select two or three of the majors you have checked to explore in more detail. Complete Exercise 4.4. (Or your instructor may wish to give you a set of questions more specific to your campus.) Interview faculty members, professional academic advisors, seniors in these majors, or others on campus who are knowledgeable about course requirements, how to declare this major, possible career relationships, and other relevant information.

EXERCISE 4.4 *Researching a Major*

Academic Major Interview

Name of academic major _____

Department/College _____

Name and title of interviewee _____

1. What *basic or general education courses* are required in this major (e.g., English, math, science, humanities, social science)?

_____

_____

_____

_____

2. What *basic courses in the major* can you take to test your interest/abilities in this area?

_____

_____

_____

_____

3. What are some *upper-level courses in this major* that sound interesting to you? (Give course number and name.)

_____

_____

_____

_____

4. What *additional courses* (e.g., perhaps in other departments) do you need to complete this major?

_____

_____

_____

_____

5. If *elective* hours are available in this major, what are some courses you might consider?

_____

_____

_____

_____

6. What is the *total number* of credit hours needed to graduate with this major? _____

Number of credit hours in the major only _____

7. What is *required to enter* this major (e.g., certain courses completed, application to a selective admission area, certain grade point average; no requirements)?

_____

_____

_____

_____

8. What *occupational or career relationships* exist for this major (e.g., accounting majors can become Certified Public Accounts; English majors can become editors or teachers; consumer affairs majors can work in business; engineering technology majors can work in industry)?

_____

_____

_____

_____

9. What are some *positive* aspects of this major, according to your interviewee? *Negative* aspects:

_____

_____

_____

_____

10. What are your *overall impressions* of this major as a potential choice for you? If positive, what are your next steps?

_____

_____

_____

_____

Academic Major Interview

Name of academic major _____

Department/College _____

Name and title of interviewee _____

1. What *basic or general education courses* are required in this major (e.g., English, math, science, humanities, social science)?

_____

_____

_____

_____

2. What *basic courses in the major* can you take to test your interest/abilities in this area?

_____

_____

_____

_____

3. What are some *upper-level courses in this major* that sound interesting to you? (Give course number and name.)

_____

_____

_____

_____

4. What *additional courses* (e.g., perhaps in other departments) do you need to complete this major?

_____

_____

_____

_____

5. If *elective* hours are available in this major, what are some courses you might consider?

_____

_____

_____

_____

6. What is the *total number* of credit hours needed to graduate with this major? _____

Number of credit hours in the major only _____

7. What is *required to enter* this major (e.g., certain courses completed, application to a selective admission area, certain grade point average; no requirements)?

_____

_____

_____

_____

8. What *occupational or career relationships* exist for this major (e.g., accounting majors can become Certified Public Accounts; English majors can become editors or teachers; consumer affairs majors can work in business; engineering technology majors can work in industry)?

_____

_____

_____

_____

9. What are some *positive* aspects of this major, according to your interviewee? *Negative* aspects:

_____

_____

_____

_____

10. What are your *overall impressions* of this major as a potential choice for you? If positive, what are your next steps?

_____

_____

_____

_____

Graduate or Professional Education

It may be worthwhile to consider extending your schooling beyond an undergraduate degree. Certain professions require extended education (e.g., medicine, actuarial science, law, licensed psychologist). As mentioned earlier, a graduate degree in some areas can open new or broader opportunities—for example, a Masters in Business Administration (MBA) and a Masters in Social Work (MSW). When considering graduate or professional school, examine your occupational goals, your academic abilities (as established by your academic record), your chances of being accepted by a graduate or professional school, and other personal factors such as your financial situation, family obligations, time constraints, or the need for geographical change.

A great deal of study and thought must go into such an important decision, and it is imperative to establish an exploratory plan to gather the information needed to make a realistic assessment. First, talk to faculty in your field of interest about the application process, excellent schools in that field, and your chances of being accepted. Books about graduate schools organized by field are available in libraries. Some computerized career information systems such as *Discover* contain information about graduate and professional programs in universities across the country. In addition, talk to individuals in the field; they will provide a different perspective about the necessity or feasibility of considering a graduate program.

After narrowing your choices to certain institutions, write to them for information about admission criteria and possible financial aid programs. Certain national examinations, such as the Graduate Record Examination (GRE), Law School Admission Test (LSAT), or Psychological Aptitude Test (PAT) may be required. Explore the need for further information about credentials, licenses, and other certification requirements in certain occupations. In some cases, continuing education may be required, but not through a graduate degree.

The *Occupational Outlook Handbook* (2000–2001) has organized the fastest-growing occupations by the level of education required (see Table 4.1). What level of education is indicated for some of the occupations you are now considering? Are any of the occupations in Table 4.1 on your list? If so, which ones?

TABLE 4.1 *Projected fastest growing occupations between 1998 and 2008 by level of education and training.*

FASTEST GROWING OCCUPATIONS	EDUCATION/TRAINING CATEGORY	OCCUPATIONS HAVING THE LARGEST NUMERICAL INCREASE IN EMPLOYMENT
Veterinarians	First-professional degree	Physicians
Chiropractors		Lawyers
Physicians		Clergy
Lawyers		Veterinarians
Clergy		Pharmacists
Biological scientists	Doctoral degree	College and university faculty
Medical scientists		Biological scientists
College and university faculty		Medical scientists
Physicists and astronomers		Physicists and astronomers
Speech-language pathologists and audiologists	Master's degree	Counselors
Physical therapists		Physical therapists
Counselors		Speech-language pathologists and audiologists
Urban and regional planners		Psychologists
Archivists, curators, and conservators		Librarians

(continued)

Continued. **TABLE 4.1**

FASTEST GROWING OCCUPATIONS	EDUCATION/TRAINING CATEGORY	OCCUPATIONS HAVING THE LARGEST NUMERICAL INCREASE IN EMPLOYMENT
Engineering, science, and computer systems managers Medical and health services managers Management analysts Artists and commercial artists Advertising, marketing, and public relations managers	Work experience plus bachelor's or higher degree	General managers and top executives Engineering, science, and computer systems managers Advertising, marketing, and public relations managers Management analysts Financial managers
Computer engineers Computer systems analysts Database administrators Physicians assistants Residential counselors	Bachelor's degree	Computer systems analysts Computer engineers Teachers, secondary school Social workers Teachers, elementary school
Computer support specialists Paralegals and legal assistants Health information technicians Physical therapy assistants and aides Respiratory therapists	Associate degree	Registered nurses Computer support specialists Paralegals and legal assistants Dental hygienists Electrical and electronic technicians and technologists
Data processing equipment repairers Surgical technologists Central office and PBX installers and repairers Emergency medical technicians Manicurists	Postsecondary vocational training	Licensed practical nurses Automotive mechanics Hairstylists and cosmetologists Emergency medical technicians Data processing equipment repairers
Private detectives and investigators Detectives and criminal investigators Instructors, adult (nonvocational) education Lawn service managers Office and administrative support supervisors	Work experience in a related occupation	Office and administrative support supervisors Marketing and sales worker supervisors Blue-collar worker supervisors Food service and lodging managers Teachers and instructors, vocational education and training
Desktop publishing specialists Correctional officers Sheriffs and deputy sheriffs Police patrol officers Telephone and cable TV line installers	Long-term on-the-job training (more than 12 months)	Correction officers Cooks, restaurant Police patrol officers Maintenance repairers, general utility Carpenters
Medical assistants Social and human services assistants Electronic semiconductor processors Dental assistants Models, demonstrators, and product promoters	Moderate-term on-the-job training (1 to 12 months)	Medical assistants Social and human services assistants Instructors and coaches, sports and physical training Dental assistants Packaging and filling machine operators
Personal care and home health aides Bill and account collectors Ambulance drivers and attendants, except emergency medical technicians Adjustment clerks Teacher assistants	Short-term on-the-job training (up to 1 month)	Retail salespersons Cashiers Truck drivers, except driver/sales workers Office clerks, general Personal care and home health aides

Source: *Occupational Outlook Handbook,* 2000–2001.

Distance Learning

Some students, particularly those with full-time jobs or other responsibilities, find it difficult to attend college in the traditional way. Distance education offers an opportunity for students who want to enroll in college but who cannot attend traditional classes on campus because of time, place, or other restrictions. Distance learning brings the classroom to the student rather than the student to the classroom. Teachers and students from different geographical locations can share information by e-mail, CD-ROM, cable television, audiographic teleconferencing, interactive satellite broadcasts, video conferencing and video imaging, or the Internet. Students may be at home, work, a library, or any predetermined location. The instructor may be located on campus.

Credit and non-credit courses, workshops, seminars, and continuing education can all be offered at a distance. If you find it difficult to attend traditional classes on campus because of work, family, or other responsibilities, you may want to explore the distance learning opportunities in your area. (An example of a website that offers a database of distance learning courses is www.lifelonglearning.com.)

Experiential Learning

You can gain important career-related learning experiences in other ways, too. Some of these are described briefly below.

Extracurricular Activities

Students have abundant opportunities to be involved in a wealth of campus activities. Student government, theatrical productions, choirs or glee clubs, residence hall councils, interest clubs, political action groups, and preprofessional organizations can offer students the opportunity to learn new skills, as well as to sharpen their managerial and leadership talents. Extracurricular activities also provide a forum for students from diverse backgrounds and cultures to learn from one another and appreciate common interests and goals. Colleges and universities offer a variety of artistic performances and engage speakers on myriad subjects. All these opportunities can add breadth and depth to students' general knowledge.

Work Experiences

In Chapter Three we discussed work experiences as one source of occupational information. The knowledge you gain from work experiences also can be useful in choosing a major. Many students work part-time during college to help pay their expenses. Your work experience can also benefit your education. You can ask co-workers about their educational background and obtain information about which academic majors are necessary or desirable for certain types of work. Some part-time or summer jobs may not require a formal education, but others do. For example, if you work as a ticket taker at an amusement park during the summer, you may want to talk to the park's business managers (if you are thinking of a business major), park designers (if you are thinking of a landscape architecture or design major), or the people who keep the park running (if you are thinking of an engineering or technical degree).

In almost any work environment you also will find occupations that do not require specific academic preparation. Some business managers, for example, have a liberal arts degree and majored in English, history, psychology, or French. Employers often do not focus on what your college major has been. They are looking for well-educated, well-rounded individuals who will work well in the specific job they seek to fill.

When you talk with co-workers about their educational backgrounds, you might ask them what college courses they feel were most useful for and applicable to their current work. In addition to educational insights, you can gain in any work setting the opportunity to observe how people work, test problem-solving skills, develop time-management skills, and learn responsibility and self-discipline. Work experiences also can measure your ability to get along with others and help you identify and clarify the educational and work values that are important to you.

In Chapter Seven you will apply work experiences you have had to the job-search process.

Internships and Cooperative Education

One of the best ways to reinforce or confirm your choice of college major is to work as an intern in an area related to your academic interests. Internships may be paid or unpaid and usually are limited to a single experience, although sometimes they may be repeated. A short-term internship is a way to gain experience in several occupational areas.

The process of applying for an internship is an excellent learning tool. Putting together a resume and interviewing for the position can be good training for a job search. If you can obtain an internship in the same city as your college, you might be able to take a lighter load of courses. The specific internship you want, however, may be located in a different geographical area. Consult with your financial aid office or other possible funding sources to see if you are eligible for a stipend. You also might obtain course credit for the experience if it relates to your academic major.

Co-operative experiences are different from internships in that they alternate an academic term with a term of paid, full-time employment. Some co-ops require a two-term, separate work commitment, although you may wish to voluntarily extend the number of terms in which you work in a co-op setting. Many companies offer co-op opportunities for the purpose of training future workers, and they may expect to make an incremental increase in the responsibilities your job entails with each additional term. A co-op position can offer you invaluable insights into how a work environment operates and how you can contribute to the mission of the work setting. A co-op experience is probably the best preparation for the job-search process because it provides you with firsthand experience in the field. Companies frequently hire co-op students who have graduated, because the hiring personnel are familiar with the quality of the student's performance.

Study Abroad

An excellent way to broaden your knowledge of and appreciation for other cultures is to take advantage of study-abroad programs that most colleges offer. You can earn academic credit for your time away, and you are exposed to new experiences. If you major in international studies, foreign languages, literature, and other humanities, you may benefit the most academically, but regardless of your major, you will return home with knowledge and memories that will last a lifetime. When you enter the job market, you will be an attractive candidate to employers who appreciate the value of exposure to other cultures and look favorably upon this unique experience.

Volunteer Work

If you are unable to take advantage of study abroad, internships, or co-ops, volunteer work will provide similar exposure in a real-world setting and will help you confirm your educational choices. Many campuses have offices with lists of volunteer sites.

The yellow pages are another source for locating types of work experiences that align with your career goals. Some organizations, such as hospitals and nursing homes, have volunteer opportunities. Frequently, a volunteer job evolves into a part-time, paid position.

> David is a television station manager who started as a volunteer—moving sets, running for coffee, and performing any "gofer" job asked of him. In time, he became such an accepted part of the staff that he was offered a part-time, paying job. David was able to confirm his interest in the communications area not only as a major but also a career. He later took an entry-level position, and eventually a managerial post.

Service Learning

Some colleges incorporate service projects into curricular or extracurricular activities. Although not new (some campuses have been using service learning for more than 20 years), learning by performing service to the campus or greater community has increased in recent years. Service learning is different from volunteering in that service learning projects are designed, supervised, and evaluated based on specific educational goals. Service projects might include service within the campus, the immediate community, or the wider community. They may be incorporated as a curricular requirement or as an academic credit course. If your campus offers service learning as an option, you may not only offer service to others or gain practical knowledge and experience but also may be able to connect your involvement to work-related activities that you can use later in the job search process.

CASE STUDY   *Jed and Maria*

EXPLORATION It never occurred to Jed that he would not go to college since his family took it for granted that he would. When he checked the reasons for attending college in Chapter Four he realized many of his reasons were personal and career related rather than academic. When he matched his interests and abilities with the matrix in Exercise 4.3, he found that Parks and Recreation Management, Physical Education, and Marketing had more than two dots. He decided to interview academic advisors in all three of these areas to find out the course requirements for these majors at his college. Since he had already interviewed a teacher and a personal fitness trainer, he decided to use the "people bank" of alumni offered by his college to interview a person working in the marketing and exercise science fields. He also decided eventually to take advantage of the college's internship program so that he could get direct work experience under supportive supervision.

When Maria accessed the *Occupational Outlook Handbook* on the Web, she also read about the education and training she would need to become a computer programmer. In her career class she matched her interests, abilities, and skills with the majors in the matrix and found that computer science appeared to be an appropriate academic major for her. She was both excited and scared. Could she do it? Did it make sense for her to embark on a difficult course of study when she had so many responsibilities? How would college affect her work and vice versa? She clearly had many factors to consider as she debated her options.

While the various types of experiences described (extracurricular activities, work experiences, internships, cooperative education, study abroad, volunteer work, and service learning) will help you make more satisfying educational choices, they also will also give you insights into potential career areas. Academic interests and early life experiences frequently stimulate interests in related occupations.

Furthermore, the amount of preparation needed for occupations such as physician, lawyer, engineer, and college professor is extensive. Are you willing to commit the time and effort required to achieve your goal? Clearly, your educational decisions are an integral part of choosing your career.

Summary Checklist

What I have learned

_____ My campus has a complete list of academic majors, and I have narrowed them down to at least three.

_____ I have examined these majors in view of my interests and abilities and have confirmed that they are realistic.

_____ I have talked to faculty and departmental academic advisors and/or seniors in these majors and know exactly what curricular requirements are necessary to complete a degree in these areas.

How I can use it

I can relate academic majors to specific career areas; I know that one major may lead to one job, many majors may lead to one job, and some jobs require no specific major.

Five

How Will I Decide?

Factors in Decision Making

Every day we make decisions. Some, such as getting up in the morning, are so automatic that we give them little thought. Others, such as buying a car, are more important and require a great deal of research, reflection, and study. Career decisions obviously call for careful thought and planning. Although everyone approaches the career decision-making process differently, you must take into account certain factors if the process is to be effective and satisfying for you. Exercises 5.1 and 5.2 require your input to discover how you make decisions.

How I Make Decisions   EXERCISE 5.1

Read the following sample decisions and consider how you would make each one (or how you made it in the past). Some might call for more than one letter.*

- Put "O" if *others* make the decision for you.
- Put "R" if the decision is so *routine* you don't even think about it.
- Put "T" if the decision requires occasional *thought*.
- Put "D" if the decision requires a lot of thought and is *difficult* to make.

SAMPLE DECISIONS   HOW I MAKE DECISIONS

1. When to get up in the morning   _____

2. What to do when I have free time   _____

3. To tell the truth   _____

4. To disagree strongly with a friend   _____

5. What to wear   _____

6. To drive faster than the speed limit   _____

7. To go to a party instead of studying   _____

8. To cope with a serious family problem   _____

9. To make an occupational choice   _____

10. To finance my education   _____

11. To attend classes   _____

12. What courses to select   _____

13. What major to choose   _____

14. To seek help with personal problems   _____

Did this activity offer insights into the way you make decisions? If so, what were they?

_____

_____

_____

_____

_____

How did you mark items 9 and 13? Why?

_____

_____

_____

_____

_____

*Adapted from H. B. Gelatt, B. Varenhorst, and R. Covey, *Deciding* (1972). New York: College Entrance Examination Board.

EXERCISE 5.2 My Lifeline

A lifeline will help you reflect on your life thus far, and key events and decisions you have made. Draw a line across a blank sheet of paper to symbolize your life. Plot points above the line to symbolize the high or rewarding times in your life, and points below the line to indicate the low points in your life. Place the corresponding age on the line. Use the symbols below to indicate the significance of these events. Include your career and personal goals, as well as the projected age at which you expect to accomplish these. Finally, draw a line connecting these points.

!   A time when I took a risk in making a decision

×   A time when I encountered an obstacle that prevented me from getting or doing what I wanted

o   A time when someone else made a critical decision for me

+   A time when I made a good decision

?   A critical decision I see coming in the future

Your lifeline is unique. No two lifelines are the same. The following is an example lifeline.

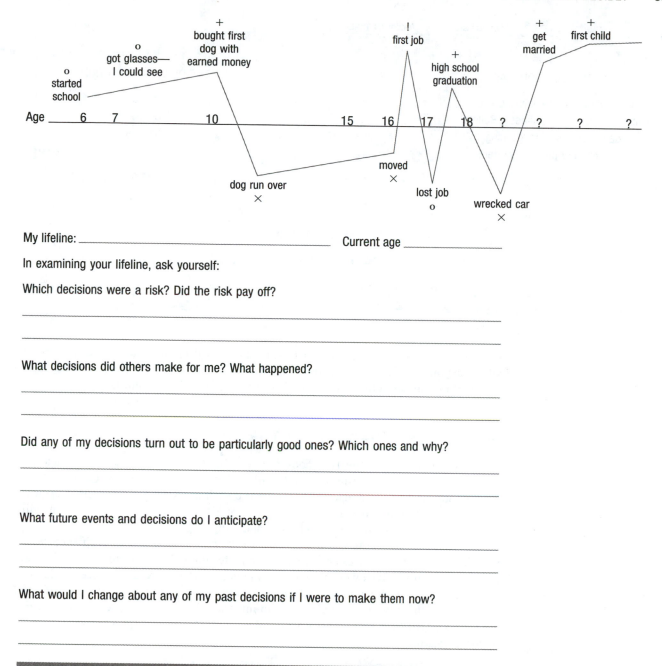

My lifeline: _____   Current age _____

In examining your lifeline, ask yourself:

Which decisions were a risk? Did the risk pay off?

_____

_____

What decisions did others make for me? What happened?

_____

_____

Did any of my decisions turn out to be particularly good ones? Which ones and why?

_____

_____

What future events and decisions do I anticipate?

_____

_____

What would I change about any of my past decisions if I were to make them now?

_____

_____

Dimensions of Decision Making

There is more to decision making than you may realize. Three basic components are especially important:

1. You as the *decision* maker
2. The *decision situation*
3. The decision-making *process*

Figure 5.1 depicts the interaction among these three parts, which we will discuss in detail next. Making decisions without considering your personal values, attitudes, and other important characteristics that make you unique will likely yield an unsat-

FIGURE 5.1   *Dimensions of decision making.*

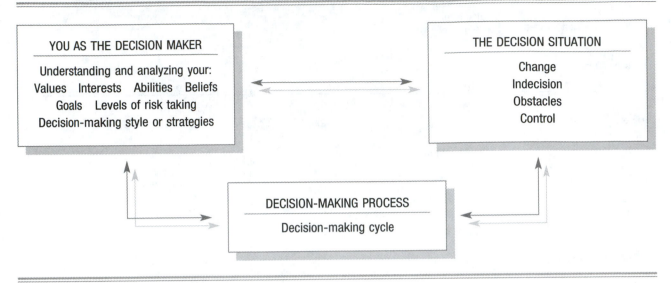

isfactory outcome. Also, each decision situation is different. You behave differently when deciding what clothes to buy than when you are choosing a major. The decision-making process consists of a logical progression of steps and tasks.

Myself as Decision Maker

As the decision maker, the first consideration should be your personal characteristics—values, interests, aptitudes, and skills—that you identified in Chapter Two. Your beliefs and feelings also influence your decisions. Knowing yourself is critical to career decision making and will lead to a productive, satisfying career that will reflect your strongest interests, aptitudes, and values.

In Chapter Two you identified your work values. These will influence your thinking as you begin to establish career and life goals. For example, if finding an occupation that involves working with people is important to you, you need to incorporate this work value into your decision-making deliberations. Simply identifying your values isn't enough. You also have to integrate them into the process. Exercises 5.3 and 5.4 will help you identify your values and how to incorporate them in your decision making.

EXERCISE 5.3   *Identifying My Values*

It is often difficult to identify your most fundamental personal and career values. This exercise might put the process into perspective and reveal the important link between you and your values. Imagine that you are 90 years old and a reporter from the local newspaper has requested an interview with you. The newspaper wants to write a feature article about you and what you accomplished during your lifetime. Write a headline for the article about yourself. (You also may want to write the article itself!)

_____

_____

_____

What does the headline tell you about your values or what is important to you in life?

_____

_____

_____

Using My Career Values in Decision Making EXERCISE 5.4

Review your personal work values from Exercises 2.4a and 2.4b in Chapter Two and write them on the lines below. Would you like to change any of them at this time? Add or change some if you wish.

_____

_____

_____

Are these work values the same or compatible with those in your headline? (If they are very different, you may want to clarify what is really important to you.)

_____

_____

_____

Review the other personal information you gathered in Chapter Two. What are your strengths (strongest skills and aptitudes)?

_____

_____

_____

What are your limitations?

_____

_____

_____

Risk Taking

Being a decision maker entails an ability or willingness to take risks. For example, you may be willing to take a risk during a card game with friends because the consequences are not going to affect your life. In a more important situation, such as how long to study for a final examination, you may be less willing to take a risk. When you make a decision, consider how much you are willing to risk, taking into account the possible good and bad consequences of the decision. For example, if you decide to buy a used car instead of a new one, you may save money, but you may have larger repair bills later. Exercise 5.5 asks you to determine whether you are or are not a risk taker.

Am I a Risk Taker?

Think about your capacity for risk taking and mark an "x" in the place on each line that best reflects where you rate yourself for that situation.

NO RISK	TO DISAGREE STRONGLY WITH YOUR BOSS	HIGH RISK
NO RISK	TO KEEP AS A PET A MONGREL DOG YOU FOUND ON THE STREET	HIGH RISK
NO RISK	TO DRIVE BEYOND THE SPEED LIMIT	HIGH RISK
NO RISK	TO JOIN THE MILITARY	HIGH RISK
NO RISK	TO CHOOSE AN ACADEMIC MAJOR	HIGH RISK
NO RISK	TO SEEK HELP CONCERNING PERSONAL PROBLEMS	HIGH RISK
NO RISK	TO CHOOSE AN OCCUPATION	HIGH RISK

Give examples of situations in which you would be willing to take a risk.

_____

_____

_____

Give examples of situations in which you would not be willing to take a risk.

_____

_____

_____

In your opinion, are you a *high, medium* or *low* risk taker? _____

How did you mark the amount of risk you would take in choosing an academic major and occupation? What does this tell you about your approach to making these decisions?

_____

_____

_____

Personal Decision-Making Style

Your personal style of decision making refers to *your approach in making decisions.* Figure 5.2 depicts the information-gathering and analysis dimensions of decision making. Researchers Johnson and Coscarelli suggest that some people may be more *spontaneous* in this process while others are more *systematic.* A spontaneous person makes a quick, intuitive decision and later tests it against information. A systematic decision maker, by contrast, feels more comfortable gathering a lot of information before making a decision and is often slower to make a commitment.

Decision-making styles. **FIGURE 5.2**

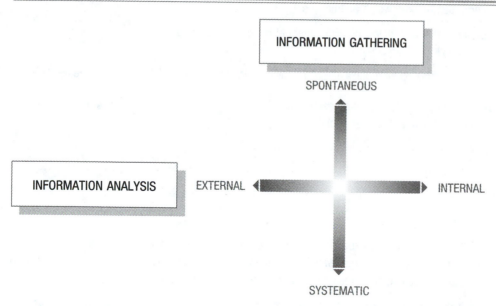

INFORMATION GATHERING

SPONTANEOUS

INFORMATION ANALYSIS

EXTERNAL · INTERNAL

SYSTEMATIC

From the *Manual for the Decision Making Inventory,* by Johnson and Coscarelli, 1983, Box 09189, Columbus, OH, 43201. Marathon Consulting and Press.

In analyzing information once it has been gathered, the *external* decision maker likes to think aloud and enjoys discussing the decision situation with friends, family, a counselor, or others before deciding. The *internal* decision maker needs to think about the information before talking to anyone about it.

When we combine these two dimensions of information gathering and analysis, we identify four distinct decision-making styles: spontaneous external, spontaneous internal, systematic external, and systematic internal. Identifying and understanding your style will help you become a more effective decision maker. For example, if you tend to be more spontaneous and external in making decisions, you probably will enjoy assignments that require talking to people in various occupations. You will engage in brainstorming and group discussions, review decisions with a classmate, or jump readily into volunteer or work experiences to test your ideas. If you tend to be more systematic and internal, you probably will enjoy reading descriptions of people in various careers; organizing your ideas in a summary grid, carefully considering the pros and cons of each alternative you identify; or using computerized career information systems to gather information in an organized way.

A number of the activities in this book ask you to respond in a systematic way; however, spontaneous decision makers will benefit from them as well. In fact, spontaneous decision makers often use systematic methods when making certain decisions. On the other hand, people with a systematic style may be uncomfortable with spontaneous methods such as class discussions, but they will benefit from hearing other students' spontaneous responses to their ideas. Exercise 5.6 is designed to elicit your decision-making style.

My Decision-Making Style   EXERCISE 5.6

Think about the approach you use when making important decisions:

I make decisions spontaneously because it feels right.   ____ yes ____ no

I make decisions systematically because I prefer to have information before I weigh alternatives.   ____ yes ____ no

I prefer to talk to people whose judgment I trust before deciding. *(externally)*   ____ yes ____ no

I prefer to think about a decision before I discuss it. *(internally)*   ____ yes ____ no

Discuss why you have chosen each dimension and how your style might have influenced your past educational and career decisions.

_____

_____

_____

_____

If you would like to examine your decision-making style in more detail, ask if your instructor can provide a copy of the *Decision Making Inventory* by Johnson and Coscarelli, or write to Marathon Consulting and Press, Box 09189, Columbus, Ohio 43201.

The Decision Situation

The decision situation incorporates the environment in which the decision is being made and all the factors involved. Sometimes you have control over elements or factors in a decision situation and other times you do not. The factors relevant to almost every decision-making situation are change, indecision, obstacles, and control.

Change

Change can occur when you least expect it and complicate a decision-making situation. It can happen before, during, or after you have made a decision, and it can even alter the outcome of a well-thought-out, planned decision. For example, you may decide to buy a used computer after you have compared its price with that of other new and used machines and after you have obtained the financing. When you call to purchase the computer, you find that it has been sold already. Your action has been thwarted (or changed) even though your original decision was sound. Expecting and adapting to change are skills we need to learn, because change is often beyond our control.

Indecision

Even though gathering information, generating alternatives, and weighing the evidence may help you reduce indecision, those efforts do not eliminate indecision entirely. A certain amount of uncertainty is to be expected in most situations, but when indecisiveness turns into procrastination, or even paralysis, it can be debilitating.

Anxiety is part of being indecisive. A little anxiety is probably helpful as it forces us to take action we might not otherwise take. Doing nothing about uncertainty may only lead to more anxiety and sometimes to lost opportunities.

When you feel uncertain about a decision, it is best to become involved in some productive activity, such as information gathering. For example, when you are deciding among two or three career choices, you might collect information about all three (e.g., by talking with workers in the field, volunteering or obtaining work experiences, or reading about those occupations).

Obstacles

You inevitably will encounter obstacles in most decision-making situations. These obstacles can be internal (of your own making) or external (those that other people or circumstances place in the situation). Exercise 5.7 is a checklist of frequent obstacles.

Checklist of Obstacles   EXERCISE 5.7

Below is a checklist of obstacles that people frequently encounter. Check (✓) those you may be facing as you attempt to make a tentative career decision.

INTERNAL OBSTACLES

_____ Fear of failure

_____ Lack of motivation

_____ Fear of making the wrong choice

_____ Lack of confidence in my skills

_____ Eliminating certain occupations because of stereotypes I hold

EXTERNAL OBSTACLES

_____ Family career pressures

_____ Poor job market when I graduate

_____ Societal barriers, (e.g., discrimination)

_____ The academic major I need is not available at my college

_____ Lack of money to pursue education and training

What other internal or external obstacles might you encounter? How would you overcome them?

_____

_____

_____

_____

_____

_____

Control

Who is in control of your career decisions? You may be tempted at times to make decisions based on someone else's wishes or desires. Although it may be easier to allow others to make decisions for you, if you depend on others for answers, you might not get the results you want. Decision makers must live with the outcomes of their choices, so they must ensure that the final decision is theirs alone. For example, if you chose premedicine as your major because your parents pressured you, but you dislike the coursework, you might resist changing majors because you feel you are letting them down.

The pressure to select a career quickly can be strong at times, but indecision about your career is not a sign of weakness. Taking some time to explore can be a positive activity that leads to a stable, satisfying decision. Feeling independent and in control is a prerequisite to effective decision making.

The Decision-Making Process

The better you understand your strengths and limitations as a decision maker in a variety of situations, the easier the decision-making process will be for you. Figure 5.3 illustrates a decision-making cycle that takes a systematic approach. Each step in this cycle is described below.

Defining the Problem

Although the critical first step in the decision-making process should be obvious, it is often ignored. First, *define what you are trying to decide.* For example, rather than trying to tackle your occupational choice all at once, break it down into its components. Rather than asking, "In what career will I spend my life?" define the problem more specifically: "What groups of occupations offer the best opportunity for me to use my love of sports?" Name the problem in specific terms. Stating the problem as a question helps to define it.

Stating the Goals

Next, state your goals. Your future expectations as they relate to your decision will influence the way you approach the other steps in the cycle. If your long-term goal, for example, is to find a job in which you can be a professional person, work for yourself, and make a high salary, you will have narrowed down considerably the information you gather and the alternatives you identify.

Setting goals is one of the most important steps in the decision-making process, as it involves projecting your values into the future. It also requires clear and critical thinking. Goal setting is a way of establishing early what you hope to accomplish by the end of the decision-making process.

Once you have made a decision (see Step 5 of Figure 5.3), check your goals and values to see if your choice has fulfilled them. If so, you are ready to take action.

Note that the vertical arrows point both ways in the cycle. Sometimes the information we collect after setting our goals (Step 3) points to directions other than those we initially considered. If this occurs, you may have to reformulate your goals in light of new or different information. In fact, your career and life goals are continually subject to change as you, your needs, or your situation changes.

Some important factors involved in goal setting are listed below. As you begin to formulate your personal and work-related goals, keep these principles in mind:

1. *Be sure that your goals are your own.* You are more likely to accomplish personal and career goals that you set for yourself than goals that others set for you.

2. *Write down your goals as clearly and concisely as possible.* Writing down your goals will make them real and available for you to review. Make a genuine commitment to strive for your goals.

3. *Begin with simple, short-term goals.* Starting with short-term and attainable goals will help you gain confidence and experience in goal setting.

4. *Consider your values as you set goals.* Goals are values projected into the future. Goal setting is easier if you clarify your values.

5. *Be sure that your goals are attainable.* Your goals should be realistic and represent a reasonable objective toward which you are willing and able to work.

6. *Set time limits for obtaining your goals.* Specifying a certain date for a goal to be accomplished will help you stay motivated and reinforce your efforts to attain it. Dates and times can and should be flexible, however, so you can change them when necessary.

You are encouraged to write your goals in Exercise 5.8.

The decision-making cycle. **FIGURE 5.3**

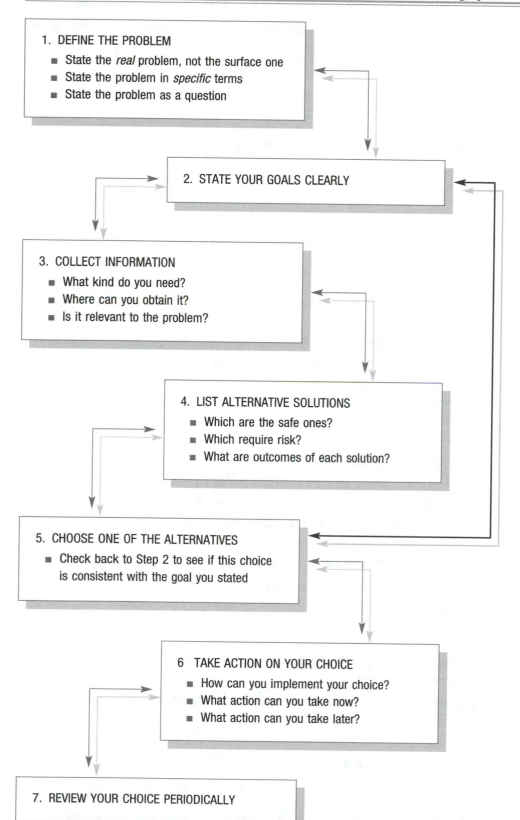

1. DEFINE THE PROBLEM

   ■ State the *real* problem, not the surface one
   ■ State the problem in *specific* terms
   ■ State the problem as a question

2. STATE YOUR GOALS CLEARLY

3. COLLECT INFORMATION

   ■ What kind do you need?
   ■ Where can you obtain it?
   ■ Is it relevant to the problem?

4. LIST ALTERNATIVE SOLUTIONS

   ■ Which are the safe ones?
   ■ Which require risk?
   ■ What are outcomes of each solution?

5. CHOOSE ONE OF THE ALTERNATIVES

   ■ Check back to Step 2 to see if this choice
     is consistent with the goal you stated

6 TAKE ACTION ON YOUR CHOICE

   ■ How can you implement your choice?
   ■ What action can you take now?
   ■ What action can you take later?

7. REVIEW YOUR CHOICE PERIODICALLY

EXERCISE 5.8   *What Are My Goals?*

Write down a school-related, short-term goal you wish to accomplish in the next several months.

_____

_____

_____

Write down a career-related, short-term goal you wish to accomplish in the next year.

_____

_____

_____

Write down a career-related, long-term goal you wish to accomplish in the next five years.

_____

_____

_____

Now examine the goals you recorded above, using the following criteria:

1. *Is my goal stated in specific terms?* (If not, rewrite it.)
   (Examples: "I want to get good grades this semester" is too general. A more specific goal is: "I want to get at least a B in chemistry this semester" or "I want to obtain a job in sales before I graduate.")

2. *Is my goal attainable?*
   - Is there enough time to accomplish the goal?
   - Am I responsible, or are there conditions beyond my control?
   - Do I have the knowledge and abilities to accomplish the goal?
   - Am I motivated enough to carry the goal to completion?
   - Do I believe in the goal?
   - Is the goal compatible with my values?

3. *How will I know when I have fulfilled my goal?*
   - What are some tangible signs?
   - What will I have accomplished?

Goal setting is important in any decision-making situation, but it is especially critical in the career decision-making process.

Collecting Information

After you have identified the decision and stated your goals, you will have to collect a great deal of information about your area of interest. You already have gathered information about your personal qualities and occupational and educational options, in Chapters Two, Three, and Four. What other information do you need? Where can you find it? Who can help you?

Listing Alternative Solutions

At this point, you should have before you many alternatives. For example, if you have collected information about professions that allow you to work for yourself and make a high salary, you may have identified medicine, law, or accounting, among others. If you examine the information you have gathered about yourself, which of the alternatives best fits your interests and abilities? Which alternatives reflect your work values? What are possible outcomes or consequences of each alternative? As you begin to integrate your self-knowledge and occupational information, you can narrow down and eliminate some of your choices. Exercise 5.9 is provided for that purpose.

Identifying Alternatives   EXERCISE 5.9

Below, write the three possible occupational alternatives identified in Exercise 3.2 in Chapter Three. List the pros and cons of each alternative.

	PROS	CONS
ALTERNATIVE 1	_____	_____
	_____	_____
	_____	_____
	_____	_____
ALTERNATIVE 2	_____	_____
	_____	_____
	_____	_____
ALTERNATIVE 3	_____	_____
	_____	_____
	_____	_____
	_____	_____

Which of your alternatives seems to be the best occupational choice?

_____

Choosing One of the Alternatives

By now one alternative may stand out so that you are ready to make a decision. Is this choice consistent with the goals you set for yourself in Step #2? Now is the time to consider the risk factors and obstacles that may prevent you from carrying out the decision.

Name of major and/or occupation I have decided upon:

_____   _____

Use this checklist to confirm your choice(s). Circle yes or no.

yes   no   This choice matches my interests as identified in Chapter Two.

yes   no   I have the abilities needed for this choice.

yes   no   This choice incorporates my work values.

yes   no   My personality seems compatible with this choice (as suggested by the Holland types discussed in Chapter Two).

yes   no   The coursework required for this choice is interesting to me.

yes   no   I have a good chance of making good grades in classes related to my choice.

yes   no   My chances of finding a job in this field are good.

yes   no   I am willing to take risks that might be associated with this choice.

yes   no   This choice will lead me to the goals I stated earlier in this chapter.

Have you answered "yes" to all the statements above? Are you ready to decide?

My choice of major and/or occupation(s) is (are):

_____   _____

Now you can proceed to the next step in the decision-making process. If you are ready, skip ahead to the section called "Taking Action on the Choice."

If you are *not* ready to make a commitment, examine the reason(s) you have circled "no." If you notice too many conflicts or cannot resolve them, you may want to return to Exercise 5.9 and identify another alternative. You also may want to complete Exercise 5.10 to help you focus on a direction.

EXERCISE 5.10   *Why Some People Don't Act on Their Decisions*

Listed below are some reasons that people don't make a commitment to their decisions. Check (✓) those that apply to you.

_____   You have made very few important decisions on your own, so you don't know how to take action.

_____   You feel it makes no difference whether you do it or not; it is out of your control.

_____   You are concerned about what others will think; maybe they will disapprove.

_____   You don't know what action steps need to be taken, so you don't know where to begin.

_____   You have not set priorities, so you don't know what to do first.

_____   You are overwhelmed by all that needs to be done, so you don't take any action.

_____   You will put it off until someone or some event forces you to take action.

_____   You are afraid of failing. What if you have made the wrong decision or taken the wrong action?

_____   You are afraid of succeeding. If you succeed you will have to deal with what comes next.

_____   You are not willing to give up immediate gratification for long-term gain.

Have you checked any of these reasons? If so, what can you do to counter them?

_____

_____

_____

If you cannot resolve the above thoughts or behaviors, you may want to consult with your instructor or a counselor for some suggestions.

Taking Action on the Choice

Once you have made a commitment to your choice, you need to take action because a decision is not finalized until you have taken action to implement it. What immediate steps can you take to set your decision in motion? (For example, if you have chosen an academic major, what do you need to do to declare this major officially?) In Exercise 5.11 you will fill out an Action Plan.

Action Plan
EXERCISE 5.11

What action will you need to take later? Devise a plan that includes action steps you will need to take in the future to implement your major and occupational choices.

Action I must take:

_____

_____

When?

_____

_____

Where?

_____

_____

How?

_____

_____

☐ Check when complete.

From the above plan, what action do you need to take first? How will you prioritize the action steps in terms of importance rather than timing? Now that you have committed to a decision and have an action plan, you will need to be aware of the last step in the decision-making process: to review your choice periodically.

Reviewing the Choice Periodically

You will need to reevaluate all your decisions on an ongoing basis. Anticipated and unanticipated changes may alter your thinking. Sometimes personal situations will force you to reconsider your ideas about work or your desired lifestyle. Accept change. Don't be afraid to change or try to anticipate change and guide it. Keep in mind your capacity to take risks. You will want to reevaluate your original decision based on actual rather than projected outcomes.

Once you have made a decision, taken action, and reviewed it, you face a series of new decisions. If you choose to become an attorney, for example, you will need to decide on a major, plan when to take the national law test (LSAT), and consider how you will pay for law school, where you wish to practice, and so forth. Exercise 5.12 may help you in decision making.

Conceptualizing decision making as a cycle will help you manage a complicated process in an orderly, rational, and timely way. As you saw in Figure 5.2, the arrows between steps go both ways. You will need to reevaluate or recycle your decision-making efforts at certain stages. If the alternative solutions you identified are not possible or desirable, you will have to collect more information and generate new alternatives. You may even have to restate your goals or redefine the decision itself in different or simpler terms.

In this chapter, you have moved through the decision-making cycle by completing the exercises. Where do you think you are in the cycle of choosing a major or a career field?

EXERCISE 5.12   *Making Decisions*

We have discussed many aspects and dimensions of the decision-making process. Think for a few moments about how you make decisions. How have you made decisions in the past?

_____

_____

_____

_____

How will you approach career decision making now?

_____

_____

_____

_____

What is different? What is the same?

_____

_____

_____

_____

What resources (e.g., friends, parents, counselors, library, workers) do you have to help you?

_____

_____

_____

_____

You now have identified your personal qualities, generated occupational and educational alternatives, and learned the factors involved in complex decisions. In Chapter Six you will learn how to gain a psychological edge and become personally effective.

CHOICE Jed is quite aware that he is not a good decision-maker. Every time he is faced with making an important decision, such as choosing an academic major, he procrastinates until people or circumstances force him to choose. He has vowed, however, that he will select an academic major by the middle of his sophomore year. Jed knows he is not a risk taker and learned in Chapter Five that he is more systematic than spontaneous in the way he approaches decisions. He also admits that he relies on other people's opinions too much, as opposed to taking responsibility for making decisions himself.

When Jed weighs the pros and cons of the choices he has considered before and during this course, majoring in physical education seems the strongest. Teaching and coaching would allow him to work with children, which he enjoys, and give him the foundation to return to school to take more academic work in any area relating to fitness if he desires. As part of his action plan, Jed learned the requirements for entering the education major at his college. His back-up plan is to major in marketing, and he is taking courses that will fulfill the requirements of both majors.

Maria believes her decision making has improved since she graduated from high school. Although she tends to be spontaneous in making decisions, working and rearing a child have resulted in her taking time and being more systematic about the decisions she makes. In thinking about what she wants to do, Maria has weighed many alternatives. She knows she is motivated and is gaining more confidence in herself as a result of actually enrolling in a college class. Maria doesn't want to do anything that will interfere with her current job success, but she realizes she must obtain new skills if she is to be financially stable.

Although finding the money for college will be a challenge, Maria does plan to seek tuition reimbursement from her employer. Her mother and father have encouraged her and have offered to take care of her daughter while Maria attends evening classes. Maria knows she has never been a risk-taker, but she realizes that now may be the time to find the courage to be one.

Summary Checklist   CHAPTER 5

What I have learned

_____ Decision making is a process in which I am constantly engaged.

_____ I have compared how I have made decisions in the past with the dimensions described in the chapter and have a better understanding of myself as a decision maker, how the decision situation presents different challenges, and how the decision-making cycle works.

_____ Having engaged in the decision-making process in this chapter, I now am able to specify at least one major or occupation that would be satisfying to me.

How I can use it

I will be able to use the decision-making skills I have learned or strengthened in this chapter in any situation that requires a systematic but intuitive approach.

How Will I Gain a Psychological Edge?

Six

Tips on Becoming Personally Effective

Whether you have been working for several years or have just begun, you are probably astonished at the number of highly skilled individuals in the workplace—individuals who seem to know more than you do and who are talented, congenial, and dedicated. With increasing competition at work, individual employees have begun searching for a psychological edge, an advantage to help them excel and be recognized as competent workers. In Chapter Five, you learned how to make effective and satisfying decisions. In this chapter, we explore the concept of personal effectiveness—personal behaviors and skills that result in enhanced performance in college, at work, and in life. Whether you are beginning your career or changing career direction, you can benefit from reflecting upon what it takes to excel.

What are the ingredients of success? During the last two decades, hundreds of books have been written with the intent of helping people improve themselves and increase their chances for success. Techniques for improving your personality, learning to communicate more effectively, and managing stress are all familiar topics to readers who avail themselves of the self-help books in their local bookstores or on the Internet. In the early 1980s, those interested in improving their performance read *Peak Performers* by Charles Garfield, and in the latter 1980s and 1990s, they read *The Seven Habits of Highly Effective People* by Stephen Covey.

Today, many books on coaching are generating a lot of attention and discussion. Professional athletes and actors have used the services of coaches for decades, and now ordinary individuals are hiring coaches to give them advice and offer strategies on how to improve their personal and professional lives.

If you study high achievers or personally effective individuals, you begin to see that they function at higher levels not because of a single talent but, rather, because certain factors, taken together, result in greater accomplishment. Some ingredients for success are discussed next.

Finding Your Mission in Life

Individuals who know what they want to do in life, who have a vision, a game plan, or a purpose or goal, are more successful than those who do not. If you have a sense of purpose, you will naturally attract those who are going in the same direction. What is your purpose or goal in life? What are you trying to achieve? Maybe you want to find a career that you will enjoy and bring you fulfillment, or maybe you want to travel and to learn about other cultures. Use Exercise 6.1 to record your life goal.

EXERCISE 6.1 *Stating a Purpose*

Take a few minutes and write your purpose in the form of a sentence. Examples are:

My purpose is to clean up the environment.

My purpose is to travel the world and study different cultures.

My purpose is to create a happy marriage and family.

My purpose is to make money and achieve security.

My purpose is

_____

_____

If writing your purpose for life seems like an overwhelming assignment, start smaller and write your goal or purpose for the year. Check your goals in Exercise 5.8, Chapter Five. Do you want to add, alter, or change any? If so write them here:

_____

_____

Replacing Distracting Things with Energy Boosters

Petty annoyances are often small irritants, but they tend to become real hassles when they are not dealt with. They drain your energy and distract you from your quest for success. Perhaps something around the house or apartment is broken, but you can't seem to get around to repairing it. Or your roommate is always leaving dishes in the sink and not doing his/her share of the cleaning.

Maybe one of your own bad habits is annoying you! Your notes are disorganized and scattered, and when it is time to study for a test, you procrastinate. Or maybe a friend has a habit of making fun of you or putting you down when you make even a small mistake. You have tolerated it but find yourself getting angrier each time it happens. Many of us tolerate petty annoyances and really don't realize how much they are irritating us, wearing us down, and draining our energy. Exercise 6.2 will help you come face to face with your distractions.

Try to get a handle on the petty annoyances in your life. Write below the things you are putting up with or tolerating that are draining your energy:

Distractions and Energy Drainers

_____	_____
_____	_____
_____	_____
_____	_____
_____	_____
_____	_____
_____	_____

Now set aside a day within the next week to tackle some of these petty annoyances. Try to eliminate everything on your list that you can. For example, sew that button or unclog the sink that is always giving you trouble. To keep yourself on task, show your list to a friend and make a bet that you can eliminate some of the more difficult things on your list by a specified date.

Some annoyances take time to eliminate. If you are having difficulty in a relationship and want to rebuild or repair it, you probably can't do it in a day. But at least you can begin. When you succeed in working through the annoyances that bother you most, you should reward yourself by going out to dinner or indulging in some other favorite activity.

Simplifying Your Life

One way to attract something new in your life is to make the space—get rid of the clutter, toss out the old magazines, clothes, and memos, and sell those old books and CDs. Ask yourself: "Have I used this in the past six months?" If your answer is no and it isn't a seasonable item, toss it. If you don't know where to start, take one room at a time. Give your usable items to your local Salvation Army or Goodwill. Someone will appreciate what has been cluttering up your space. Getting rid of things you do not need can invigorate you and create the sensation of starting anew.

Once you have rid yourself of the clutter in your life, look at your schedule. If your schedule is packed with stuff to do, people to meet, and places to go, it may be time to simplify. People who are too busy can miss opportunities because they don't notice what is going on around them and don't have time to think. Consolidate your credit cards so you don't spend so much time paying and keeping track of bills. Drop call-waiting from your telephone. Before you say yes to a social event, make certain it is really something you want to do.

Managing Your Time Effectively

Do you attend classes, study as hard as you can, and then run to your part-time or full-time job? Do you find yourself complaining that there aren't enough hours in the day? If you feel pressed for time, perhaps you should take a week and track your time in one-hour increments. Keep a notepad in your pocket or bookbag and write down what you are doing each hour from the time you rise until you go to bed. Writing just a few words will allow you to keep track of how you are spending your time. At the end of the week, quickly calculate how much time you spend on major life activities. Exercise 6.3 is a time log for you to use in recording how you spend your time.

EXERCISE 6.3 *Time Log*

ACTIVITIES

AMOUNT OF TIME SPENT
IN ONE WEEK (168 HOURS)

1. Commuting to college _____
2. Commuting to work _____
3. Walking across campus _____
4. Attending class _____
5. Studying _____
6. Talking on the phone _____
7. Sleeping _____
8. Working _____
9. Watching television _____
10. Listening to CDs _____
11. Hanging around with my friends _____
12. E-mail or Internet _____
13. ? _____
14. ? _____

Are you surprised by how you spend your time? If yes, why?

_____

In what areas do you think you are wasting time?

_____

Is the way you are spending your time now the way you want to spend your time? If not, how do you plan to reschedule your time so you will use it more effectively in school, work, and life?

_____
_____
_____
_____

Learning to Say No

Are you overcommitted with work and social obligations? Do you find yourself participating in activities that don't really interest you? Perhaps you need to learn to say no. Women in particular are brought up in our society to please and to be liked. As a result of this kind of socialization, they find it harder to say no when asked to do favors or take on extra work. Some fear that saying no will turn off their friends, but in reality it doesn't. Often your friends and colleagues respect you more when they learn they cannot take advantage of you. Learning to say no is one way of getting control of your time and your life.

Managing Your Money Well

During the last 20 years, it has become acceptable to have debts. Your parents probably saved money before they purchased a cherished item, whereas you may find it easy to simply charge the cost to your credit card. The costs of immediate gratification (charge it now) can be high. First, the interest rate on debt is high. Second, too much debt can lead to stress that can drain your energy, making it difficult for you to be your best and attract the people and opportunities you want. Instead if you pay off the balance on your credit cards each month, you will feel lighter, more free, and in control of your life.

Building a Strong Network of Friends

Part of your success in life and work is having some close friends with whom you can laugh, love, and celebrate your and their successes. Be aware of the people around you, and get to know those who are particularly interesting. With our increased mobility, we sometimes have to create our own communities, a circle of friends with whom we feel comfortable and supported. Some create this circle of friends at college or at work, and others find opportunities to create friendships at church or in clubs. Be proactive and create your own network of friends.

Making Time for Yourself

Life can become boring if we do not have something to look forward to. Taking a walk, reading the paper, talking to friends or your spouse, taking a hot bubble bath, or listening to your favorite music—these are just a few examples of activities that might be pleasurable and inspiring to you. Exercise 6.4 encourages you to make more time for yourself.

Taking Time for Myself   EXERCISE 6.4

Taking time for and enjoying yourself is an important way to keep balanced in today's hectic world. List four or five activities that you really look forward to doing:

_____

_____

_____

_____

_____

When was the last time you took time to do the activities you listed?

_____

What can you change in your schedule to give you the time to do something for yourself every day?

_____

The tips suggested so far in this chapter not only will make you more effective but will help you enjoy life as well. Several additional skills will help you to be successful in your work. The discussion now will turn to those skills: communicating effectively, managing stress, and accepting and adapting to change.

Communicating Effectively

In the work world of today and the future, employees work together on teams, collaborating with others to solve problems or to create new products and services. Collaborating, or teaming, requires good communication skills. Employees who already possess effective communication skills will have an edge over those who don't. You can develop the skills discussed next to improve your communication with fellow students, professors, friends, family members, and co-workers.

Effective communication entails constructing and sending clear messages. It also involves receiving messages accurately.

Constructing a Clear Message

Misunderstandings can occur when speakers fail to communicate effectively. Saying exactly what you mean is not always easy. You must think about the message you want to send. Your message should be clear and concise. It is wise to "put your mind in gear before opening your mouth."

Sending and Receiving Skills

In his book *Human Relations and Your Career* (1987), David Johnson describes what he considers to be basic *sending skills* (those that help you send a message) and *receiving skills* (those that help you truly hear the message being sent). These skills can help you improve your communication.

The following are sending skills.

1. *Speak for yourself.* You speak for yourself when you use the pronouns *I, me, my,* and *mine.* You take ownership of your ideas, needs, and feelings when you say, "I think . . .," "I feel . . .," and "I want . . . ." The more you speak for yourself, the clearer your messages will be. The less you speak for yourself, the more confused and confusing your messages will be. For example, saying "I don't understand the directions" is clear. You have owned your statement. On the other hand, saying "Some people say the directions are not clear" is confusing. Who is saying "the directions are not clear"?

2. *Describe, don't judge.* Judgments and generalities impede effective communication. They usually anger the receiver. If the receiver feels defensive, further communication is often negative. When discussing other persons and situations, *describe* behavior; don't make judgments about them. Say, "She was five minutes late for work today" rather than "She is a lazy person who never arrives on time."

3. *Use effective relationship statements.* How well two people work together depends on how good their relationship is. With some people, you feel compatible almost immediately. With others, you have to work at building and maintaining a good relationship. Sometimes conflicts arise between you and co-workers or friends. When this happens, sit down and discuss the problems in your relationship. Make "relationship statements," which describe how you see the relationship or some aspect of it. Relationship statements focus on the relationship, not on the other person. "I appreciate your listening to me carefully so I can tell you about the frustration I'm feeling" is an example of a good relationship statement because it indicates clear ownership and describes without judging. On the other hand, a poor relationship statement speaks for the other person and makes judgments about the relationship.

4. *Consider the perspective of others.* Misunderstandings often arise because each of us assumes that everyone else sees things from our perspective. The same message can mean two different things to two different people. When you send a message, you need to consider the receiver's perspective, what the receiver knows about the issue, and what further information the receiver needs about the issue. By taking these factors into account, you can phrase your message more accurately.

5. *Pay attention to nonverbal cues.* Every face-to-face communication is influenced by your nonverbal behaviors. Your tone of voice, amount of eye contact, distance between you and the person(s) receiving your message, and your facial expression are all parts of your message. If you send a message that is meant to be supportive, your facial expression and tone of voice also must be supportive. As much as 60 percent of communication is nonverbal; therefore, appropriate use of nonverbal skills is essential.

Communication is a two-way street. In addition to constructing and sending clear messages, listen to receive messages accurately. Some effective receiving skills are described below.

1. *Become a good listener.* Stop talking. You cannot listen if you are always talking. Listening is a powerful tool. When you listen to what people say, you make them feel important. Several tips for good listening are as follows.

- Look directly at the person who is speaking. Good eye contact is important.
- Avoid letting your own thoughts preoccupy you. Don't rush ahead with your own thoughts; pay attention to the nonverbal cues (tone of voice, facial expression, body gestures) the speaker is giving you.
- Try to listen for more than just the spoken words to determine how those talking perceive themselves.
- Say something to the speaker (paraphrase what has been said, if appropriate) or nod your head to communicate that you are following the conversation.
- Don't judge the person but, rather, accept what is said. Accepting speakers will help them feel comfortable enough to continue talking.

2. *Paraphrase accurately.* Restating in your own words what another person says and what you think the person feels and means improves communication in several ways. *First,* it helps you avoid judging and evaluating. When you are restating, you are not passing judgment. *Second,* restating gives the sender direct feedback on how well you understand the message. If you do not fully understand, the sender can revise the message. If you are misinterpreting the meaning of the message, the sender can clarify. Clarifying and elaborating are important ways to ensure good communication. *Third,* paraphrasing communicates to the sender that you want to understand the message. It shows you care enough to listen. *Fourth,* paraphrasing helps you see the message from the sender's perspective. When paraphrasing includes feelings, the communication sometimes becomes more difficult. Listen carefully.

3. *Pay attention to the sender's nonverbal cues.*   Sometimes senders use nonverbal cues that communicate a lot of feelings. Listen for feelings. Sometimes the sender's words communicate one thing while the nonverbal expression of feelings communicates another. Also observe the sender's tone of voice (is it soft, loud, harsh, normal?); eyes (is the sender making contact with you?); facial expression (is the sender's expression congruent with the message being sent?); and gestures (are the gestures relaxed or tense?). Exercise 6.5 will get you started on improving your communication skills.

How do you assess your communication skills?

EXERCISE 6.5   *Improving My Communication Skills*

Briefly describe a current situation in which you are having difficulty communicating with another person:

_____

_____

_____

_____

_____

_____

Which of the skills mentioned above might help improve that situation?

_____

_____

_____

_____

_____

Try out the skills you listed to see if they do improve the situation.

Identifying and Managing Stress

Ineffective or poor communication skills interfere with your personal effectiveness and can lead to excessive stress. Although some stress is simply a part of living in a challenging world, excessive stress can drain your energy and impede your performance.

If you are to become truly effective, you must begin to identify the sources of stress in your life and learn to manage stress at work, school, and home. Stress can be either a positive or a negative force. It is negative when it interferes with your ability to function at your optimal level. It is positive when it enhances your performance or your effectiveness. That is the key to stress management.

What does the term *stress* really mean? According to psychologist Seymour Sarason, you experience stress when you appraise an event (a demand on you, a constraint, an opportunity, or a challenge) as having the potential to exceed the resources you have available. You may think it's too hard, too frightening, too challenging. Stressors, or events that can create anxiety, vary greatly from individual to individual. Three classifications are:

- *external* physical stimuli, such as heat, cold, crowding, loud noises
- *interpersonal* difficulties with others
- *internal* stimuli, such as our own thoughts or feelings

Although stressors are specific to individuals to some extent, universal categories of stressors are: environmental stressors, life stress events, and daily hassles.

Environmental stressors include things such as noise, crowding, commuting time, worry about crime, traffic and pollution, economic difficulties, isolation, restricted leisure opportunities, and job insecurity. These often are a function of where you live and sometimes your socioeconomic class.

Life stress events are major occurrences that create stress and require people to change and adapt. Holmes and Rahe (1967) identified 43 life events that cause significant stress and assigned each event a weight, using what they called "life change units." Events that call for a greater amount of change and adaptation are assigned a higher number of life change units. For example, the death of a spouse is assigned a very high weight. Holmes and Rahe used their instrument, the Social Readjustment Rating Scale, to measure the amount of life stress a person was experiencing. They found that too many life stress events forced the body to adapt and change so much that those stresses weakened the immune system.

In fact, researchers have made connections between life stress events and both physical and mental illness. Evidence has shown that life stress events contribute to emotional disorders, heart disease, accidents, and other conditions. Whether individuals who experience stressful life events subsequently become ill, however, also depends on their personal vulnerability, as well as the amount of social and emotional support available to them.

Daily hassles (for instance, physical appearance, concerns about weight, too many things to do, and losing or misplacing things) are also stressors. Until the early 1980s, little research had been done on the effect of minor but more common daily hassles. Since then, researchers have paid considerable attention to studying the effects of hassles on health. Hassles seem to vary depending on age and, to some extent, the circumstances in which people find themselves. Common daily hassles for students are:

Taking tests or exams

Worrying about not meeting academic deadlines

Not knowing how to study effectively

Taking hard and demanding classes

What other stressors are you dealing with in school and life? Exercise 6.6 will help you identify your sources of stress.

Identifying Stressors in My Life   EXERCISE 6.6

Circle the number on the following scale that best describes your reaction:

    0—not a source of stress   1—mildly stressful
    2—moderately stressful   3—very stressful

COLLEGE/WORK

0 1 2 3   I have too many demands on me.
0 1 2 3   I don't like my current choice of academic major.
0 1 2 3   I'm unsure of my responsibilities at my job.

0   1   2   3   I'm not able to handle my college courses as well as I should.

0   1   2   3   My communication with a supervisor or professor is not good.

0   1   2   3   My salary is not sufficient to pay my bills.

ENVIRONMENTAL

0   1   2   3   My work/home environment is not pleasant.

0   1   2   3   I'm concerned about crime and how it affects my safety.

0   1   2   3   I'm concerned about pollution.

0   1   2   3   I'm bothered by the noise around me.

0   1   2   3   I don't like my daily commute.

LIFE EVENTS

0   1   2   3   During the last year, I changed my academic major/job.

0   1   2   3   My partner and I just broke up.

0   1   2   3   I recently suffered a personal injury or illness.

0   1   2   3   I failed a course or lost a job in the last 12 months.

0   1   2   3   I have had a sexual problem within the last year.

0   1   2   3   I changed my residence at least once this year.

0   1   2   3   One of my parents has been sick during the last year.

DAILY HASSLES

0   1   2   3   I feel my family's expectations of me are too great.

0   1   2   3   I don't seem to organize my time well.

0   1   2   3   I worry about transportation to and from campus.

0   1   2   3   I have problems with my roommates.

0   1   2   3   I worry about speaking in class.

0   1   2   3   My professors' expectations of me are too high.

0   1   2   3   I never seem to have any time to relax.

FINANCES

0   1   2   3   I'm concerned about job security.

0   1   2   3   My salary is not enough to meet my monthly expenses.

0   1   2   3   I've made a large purchase (e.g., house, car, computer).

0   1   2   3   I don't have enough money for recreation and leisure.

HEALTH

0   1   2   3   I'm concerned about my weight.

0   1   2   3   I'm concerned about my physical fitness.

0   1   2   3   I have been smoking, drinking, or using drugs excessively.

0   1   2   3   I have been eating excessively.

0   1   2   3   I'm concerned about my general health.

List any additional sources of stress in your life:

_____

_____

_____

_____

_____

(Circle one.) Reviewing your responses, would you characterize yourself as experiencing:

(a) little stress

(b) moderate stress

(c) excessive stress?

If you circled moderate or excessive stress, you will want to read the suggestions that follow.

Strategies for Managing Stress

Some strategies are available to help you manage stress so it does not become excessive and interfere with your performance. You will learn several techniques that you can apply to your life now.

Relaxing

Preventive approaches such as relaxation training are important to any stress management program. The term *relaxation training* refers to any of several techniques whose purpose is to decrease the negative symptoms the human body experiences under stress. The premise behind relaxation is this: If individuals can be taught to relax, they should be able to produce voluntarily an alternative physiological response to offset the negative stress symptoms. For example, if a stress reaction results in increases in muscle tension, blood pressure, or heart rate, the voluntarily induced state of relaxation can reverse these increases.

One of the oldest relaxation techniques is *meditation*. Meditation requires that individuals engage in regular periods of rest and silence. You can find numerous books and workshops addressing the different forms of meditation. Regardless of the form the meditation takes, the following four components are typically included (all four are important for beginners):

1. a quiet place, free from distractions
2. a comfortable position in which you can consciously relax your muscles
3. a mental device, such as the neutral word "one" (focus on the word rather than your thoughts)
4. a passive attitude (a relaxed rather than a tense attitude)

Have you ever meditated? Try it in Exercise 6.7.

Learning to Relax   EXERCISE 6.7

Find a comfortable position in a quiet room. Pick a word to focus on and do your best to adopt a passive attitude. Close your eyes, sit quietly, and breathe deeply for roughly 15 minutes. After finishing, briefly describe how you feel.

_____

_____

If just sitting quietly had a relaxing effect on you, you may want to learn formally how to meditate. The counseling center at your university or college may have someone trained in meditation. Contact that person for further information. You will need to practice meditation many times before you begin to feel totally comfortable with the technique.

Practicing Healthy Habits

Engaging in a healthy lifestyle goes a long way in managing stress. Individuals who experience the physiological effects of stress are endangering their health. If they also are practicing unhealthy habits that weaken the body's ability to resist stress, their level of stress may increase. Clearly, if you are stressed, you should practice good eating habits, use alcohol only moderately if at all, not smoke, and get regular exercise.

Altering Negative Attitudes and Self-Talk

Many researchers—for example, Albert Ellis, Aaron Beck (1976), and Donald Meichenbaum (1986)—have studied the role that mental attitudes and self-talk (the things you say to yourself) play in how you cope with stress. In the case of stress and stress-related problems, your view of the world and yourself influences

1. how you interpret any situation and whether you label it stressful
2. your interpretation of the consequences of the potentially stressful situation
3. your view of your own ability to cope with a potentially stressful situation

Experts on stress believe that a negative attitude or negative self-talk often increases the tension you feel during a difficult situation. These experts believe that if you work on changing your patterns of self-defeating attitudes and negative self-talk, you can reduce your stress.

Negative self-talk can become almost automatic. You cannot easily replace it with positive self-talk. If you want to reduce your stress or cope with it more effectively, become aware of when you use negative self-talk. Think about the times you are self-critical or angry with yourself. The negative self-talk you use often can be traced to attitudes or thoughts that have been distorted in some way. Most of us are simply not aware of how often we engage in distorted thinking. Typical distortions and examples of negative self-talk that might accompany each distortion are as follows.

- *All-or-nothing thinking.* You see things in black and white. If your performance falls short of perfect, you see yourself as a total failure. Example: "Just look at how I messed up this job interview. I knew I wouldn't be good at it."
- *Overgeneralization.* You see a single negative event as one in a series of never-ending defeats. Example: "Oh, no! I didn't lose my two pounds this week. I'll never be able to lose the weight I want to. I might as well quit trying."
- *Disqualifying the positive.* You reject positive experiences by insisting they don't count. You maintain negative beliefs even though your experience contradicts them. Example: "Sure, I aced this test, but it was probably just luck. I know I won't do it again."
- *Magnification.* You exaggerate the importance of something (your mistake or someone else's achievement) or minimize things until they appear insignificant (your own accomplishments). Example: "Betty and I worked on this together. We did well, but Betty deserves the credit because she was under more pressure than I was."
- *"Should" statements.* You try to convince yourself with "shoulds" and "shouldn'ts" and pressure yourself before you are expected to do something. Example: "I should finish this job before I go to the game or I'll feel guilty tomorrow."
- *Labeling.* This is a form of overgeneralization. In addition to describing your mistake, you attach a negative label to yourself. Example: "I'll never get into the major I want. I'm just a failure."

■ *Personalization.* You see yourself as the cause of some external event for which you were not responsible. Example: Another person is hired in your department. You say, "The boss probably hired the new person because I wasn't getting my work done."

In Exercise 6.8, you will analyze your own thinking distortions.

Is My Thinking Distorted?   EXERCISE 6.8

From the list of typical distortions, which ones do you use most often (e.g., personalization)?

_____

_____

_____

_____

Write down some of the specific negative statements you say to yourself:

_____

_____

_____

_____

What can you do to replace negative self-statements with positive ones? *Self-statements* (thoughts you say to yourself) are sometimes referred to as your "inner dialogue." As you have seen, negative or maladaptive self-statements, can increase your stress. Learning to change negative attitudes and self-statements gives you one more tool to use in managing stress. Psychologist Donald Meichenbaum (1986) devised a three-step self-instructional approach to help you change your negative attitudes and self-statements.

Step 1: Observe yourself. First, learn to observe your own behavior and listen to yourself. Increase your sensitivity to your thoughts, feelings, actions, physiologic reactions, and other ways of reacting to others. You must be aware of your attitudes and thoughts before you can change them.

Step 2: Begin new attitudes/self-statements. Change your self-statements or negative inner dialogue to new, positive inner dialogue, which serves as a guide to developing new behavior. As you become more aware of harmful self-statements, watch for opportunities to create positive alternative statements. For example, suppose you say to yourself, "Exercise really doesn't do me any good." You can practice replacing this negative self-statement with a more positive one such as, "I'll feel relaxed after I exercise." Positive self-statements can change the way you feel and think about yourself, your actions, and ultimately your behavior.

Step 3: Practice your new self-statements. The third step of this self-instructional process involves practicing and using your new, positive self-statements in real-life situations. Taking the example in Step 2, you would repeat the positive self-statement 10 times before and during each exercise period. The result? As the new, positive attitude and self-statement replaces the former, negative one, you will begin to believe that exercise relaxes you. Exercise 6.9 is designed to help you change your negative self-statements.

EXERCISE 6.9 *Changing My Negative Self-Statements*

Choose one of your negative self-statements from Exercise 6.8. Using the three-step self-instructional approach just described, turn that negative self-statement into a positive one and write it below.

_____

_____

_____

Practice this positive self-statement over the next several days and weeks to see if you can change your own thinking.

Meditating, practicing healthy lifestyle habits, and altering your distorted thinking and negative self-statements are three key strategies for managing stress. Excessive stress diminishes your capacity to function and can even lead to illness. On the other hand, stress can be a positive force in life and sometimes drives us to function more effectively. Stress can stimulate growth and nurture creativity. Managing stress is simply learning to cope effectively; it requires commitment and is part of a personal renewal process.

Accepting and Adapting to Change

Change is anything that causes us to shift from old and familiar ways or situations to ones that are new, different, and often challenging. More than a decade ago, Alvin Toffler talked about "waves of change" that are accelerating at a faster and faster pace. The rate of change in today's world is greater than at any time in our history. Global competition, almost unbelievable advances in technology, particularly communication technologies, and a knowledge and information explosion all contribute to this fast-paced change. Learning how to adapt and adjust to change is a critical skill that can be learned.

Self-Defeating Responses to Change

Individuals respond to change in various ways. Some people respond in self-defeating ways:

- Some try to avoid or ignore change. By ignoring the situation, they think it will disappear. They feel great anxiety or discomfort when faced with the prospect of change.
- Some deal with change by complaining about it. Some look for others who also are complainers and commiserate with them. They expend energy trying to figure out how to resist change rather than developing ways of dealing with it.
- Some react to change with little planning. They don't resist change, but they change reluctantly and with little thought about how the change could benefit them.

In the workplace, changes can be threatening. Employees fear that change will result in

heavier workloads
an inability to meet new goals and expectations

loss of position, influence, or control

denied future possibilities for advancement

instability of the job itself.

Some workers report feeling anxiety, anger, grief, resentment, and confusion. Others seem to be rejuvenated by the possibility of new responsibilities and challenges.

At times, change can create situations in which you feel you have little or no control over events going on around you. When that happens, we usually experience anxiety or stress. Although we cannot always control what is happening in our life or at work, we can control our reaction to it. We can decide how to react to change so it does not overwhelm us.

Strategies for Dealing with Change

In times of rapid change, you must be able to adapt quickly. Below are several suggestions on how to adapt to change rather than ignore or resist it:

- Withhold judgment and tolerate ambiguity or uncertainty until you see the results of whatever change you are experiencing.
- Be flexible and try new approaches.
- Keep current about changes and trends in your field and try to understand their potential impact.
- Anticipate the new skills needed in your field and acquire them.
- View change as part of a natural process of growth.
- Look to the future; don't glorify the past beyond its worth.
- Scan your environment and reassess your goals regularly.

    Exercise 6.10 gives you an opportunity to apply these strategies to your own life.

Adapting to Change   EXERCISE 6.10

List three changes that have occurred in your life or at work in the last 18 months:

1. _____

2. _____

3. _____

    Circle the responses to change below that you used when you experienced the change.

1. I avoided change at all costs.

2. I complained about change.

3. I reluctantly changed.

4. I saw change as an opportunity and developed ways to deal with it.

Were your responses to change the same in all situations? Why or why not?

_____

_____

_____

_____

Would you respond differently to any one of the situations now? Why or why not?

_____

_____

_____

_____

Ethical Behavior

Take stock of your interactions and behavior at work and school. Observe how others react to what you say and do. Standards of conduct at work are considerably higher now than a decade ago. Business people and the public expect more sensitive behavior now.

Sometimes individuals do not seem to think about how their behavior negatively influences others. Others do not seem to care. They appear to be unprepared to deal with the complexities of respecting those with whom they work. To encourage you to reflect on the impact of your behavior in the work environment, we have developed three case studies to which you will respond in Exercise 6.11. In 6.12 you are asked to identify unethical behaviors.

EXERCISE 6.11   *Making Ethical Choices*

Read the case studies and decide whether the behavior is appropriate and ethical. Write your responses.

Case Study #1.   Janet is revising her resume two months prior to graduation, and she knows that many employers like to see a grade point average of 3.00 or above. Her cumulative GPA at graduation probably will be over 3.00 as she is doing well in her classes. But it is currently 2.93. Should Janet list her GPA as 2.93 or as 3.12 (averaging her expected grades)?

_____

_____

_____

_____

Case Study #2.   Jaime is applying for a position that has all the elements of his ideal job. He meets all the requirements for this position—except one. It calls for a bachelor's degree, but he will not receive his for another year. This kind of job comes along only once in a lifetime, Jaime thinks, so he has decided to write on his resume that he has already received his college degree. Do you think this is acceptable? Why or why not?

_____

_____

_____

_____

Case Study #3. Maya is a demanding supervisor. She has worked at the same company as you for 20 years and takes great pride in her work. John, one of your co-workers, believes Maya expects too much. He is always putting her down. Is John's behavior ethical? Why or why not? Can you suggest another way he might deal with this situation?

_____

_____

_____

_____

_____

Identifying Unethical Behaviors

EXERCISE 6.12

Review carefully the following lists of sample unethical school and work behaviors, then answer the questions.

UNETHICAL SCHOOL BEHAVIORS

- copying others' homework
- cheating on a test
- plagiarizing another's work
- misusing your college identification card
- making up an excuse for a late assignment
- taking an examination for someone else
- pilfering a new pencil from the bookstore

UNETHICAL WORK BEHAVIORS

- adding several minutes to your time sheet
- covering for a co-worker who is late
- lying about something you have or haven't done
- lying to cover for an undependable co-worker.
- trying to embarrass a co-worker or get her in trouble with the boss
- telling off-color stories, though you know it makes some people feel uncomfortable
- touching or teasing one of your co-workers when it is clear the behavior is unwanted
- gossiping about other employees or your boss
- letting an inferior product go out the door although you know it may break or isn't good quality
- stealing something from work
- making fun of someone or putting him down because of race, gender, religion, or ethnicity

Do you agree that the lists of behaviors above are examples of unethical behavior at school and/or work? _____ If so, which behaviors are most troublesome to you? Why?

_____

_____

_____

_____

What other unethical behaviors have you observed at school or work?

_____

_____

_____

_____

How did you react?

_____

_____

_____

_____

Now it is time to put the ideas in this chapter all together by trying to answer the question: How personally effective am I? Complete the Peak Effectiveness Checklist in Exercise 6.13 to assess your strengths and identify areas in which you need to improve.

EXERCISE 6.13   *Peak Effectiveness Checklist*

Place a checkmark (✓) next to those qualities and characteristics that best describe you.

_____ I accept responsibility for my own life.

_____ I see change as a source of opportunity and guide it.

_____ I start with a clear direction.

_____ I set priorities and have the discipline to carry them out.

_____ I concentrate on solving problems and not placing blame.

_____ I believe that solutions should be mutually beneficial.

_____ I value differences and build on them.

_____ I listen and try to understand others.

_____ I know when I am feeling excessive stress.

_____ I practice meditation or healthy lifestyle habits, or both.

_____ I change my negative self-talk into positive thoughts and statements.

_____ I look at the person who is speaking.

_____ I listen without my thoughts rambling.

_____ I observe the speaker's nonverbal cues.

_____ I listen for more than just someone's spoken words.

_____ I try not to judge the speaker but, rather, accept what is said.

_____ I paraphrase or restate to seek clarification.

_____ I act in a genuine and caring way.

_____ I respect others.

_____ I try to remain open to others' values and experiences.

_____ I understand how my values influence me.

_____ I engage in ethical behavior in my personal and work life.

What are four of your strengths?

1. _____   3. _____

2. _____   4. _____

What four areas do you believe you need to improve?

1. _____   3. _____

2. _____   4. _____

Would you describe yourself as being personally effective?

_____ yes _____ no

Why or why not?

_____

_____

_____

_____

_____

_____

_____

_____

Based on what you have learned in this chapter, write your personal mission statement.

_____

_____

_____

_____

_____

_____

_____

_____

_____

_____

_____

_____

Jed and Maria

COMMITMENT Jed began to appreciate the importance of acquiring skills in college that would be transferable to the work world after graduation. He listed his habits that he believed would detract from being his best. Managing his time effectively was one habit that he needed to work on. He also decided to take a communication course to improve his speaking and listening skills. Jed realized that he did not always manage stress as well as he should, and he vowed to follow the tips in the chapter. Overall, Jed felt positive about himself, but he knew he needed to improve in some areas.

As Maria read about becoming more personally effective, she felt proud of herself. She remembered when she didn't have a direction in life and seemed to feel anxious all the time. After her divorce, she took stock of her life and began to search for ways to improve herself. She took advantage of some communication workshops at her workplace and began to feel more confident in her relationships with her co-workers. Now she is more settled and has learned to talk to herself when she feels stressed by daily hassles. She realizes that she is a good problem-solver and can adapt to change fairly easily. Although she realizes she still has a lot to learn, Maria feels ready to take advantage of every opportunity that will help her reach her goals.

This chapter has focused on personal characteristics and skills that can give you the psychological edge in school, work, and life in general. As you establish your career goals and prepare for your role of worker, continually developing these characteristics and skills can enhance your success in all areas of life. Now we return to some specific skills you will need to conduct a successful job search—resume writing, interviewing, and follow-up.

CHAPTER 6 *Summary Checklist*

What I have learned

_____ Some of my behaviors detract from my quality of living, and I have devised a plan to change those behaviors.

_____ I have analyzed my ways of communicating with others and practiced ways to improve this critical skill.

_____ I have examined some of the causes of stress in my life and practiced ways of alleviating them.

How I can use it

I must continue to improve my work habits through practice and engage in new experiences that will help me develop the skills I need to become a peak performer.

How Will I Advance My Career?

Seven

THE JOB SEARCH AND RESUME WRITING

Selling Yourself

In Chapter Three you learned about the workplace of the future and how to prepare for your role as a worker, and in Chapter Six you learned how to gain a psychological edge in the workplace. This chapter focuses on the skills you will need to continue your career planning so you ultimately will obtain your ideal job. Whether this job is your first "real" one or another in a series, you can benefit from certain skills that are relevant to any effective job search. Because experts project that you probably will change jobs as many as six times during your life, once you learn these skills, you can use them throughout your career.

The job-search process can be both exhilarating and difficult. You will need to plan carefully, with determination, flexibility, and an honest appraisal of who you are and where you are going. Selling yourself is not a comfortable prospect for everyone, but to succeed you must believe in your ability to be an exceptional contributor to an organization and be prepared to market yourself with that attitude and belief. The main prerequisites are to know your strengths, know what you want, and be willing to spend the time and energy to enter the search process with knowledge and enthusiasm.

Ample help is available for you to learn the skills required to mount a productive job search. Many colleges have career planning and placement services that can help you develop specific job-search tools. Once you have started your search, you can seek the guidance of campus experts about how to write a resume, become an effective interviewer, follow up after an interview, and manage job offers.

Taking Action Steps

Some students wait until their senior year before they think about finding a job. Actually, you should begin to build your resume as a freshman. Picturing how you will look on paper in two, four, or more years will help you decide the kind of knowledge, skills, and experiences you will need to acquire during college. In this way, you are taking control of your future by beginning to formulate a career plan that will lead you to graduation and beyond. The following action steps are arranged by academic year. Later in this chapter you will learn how to accomplish many of these tasks.

WHAT CAN FIRST-YEAR STUDENTS DO?

Check the items you still need to do.

_____ Concentrate on learning how to study, write papers, take tests, and manage your time so you can become a successful student.

_____ Scope out campus activities (e.g., student government, chess club, symphonic choir) that match your interests, and join at least one.

_____ Select courses wisely, using the help of your academic advisor to explore possible majors.

_____ Use informational interviews to choose a major or confirm one.

_____ Begin early to make contacts and develop a resume to help you land a good summer job after your freshman year, or if you are employed full-time, think about how you can improve your job or how it matches your long-term career goals.

_____ If you are not computer-literate, now is the time to take courses to learn or to improve your skills in this area.

_____ Purchase a large folder and label it "Job Search Information." In the folder put everything you collect related to future jobs.

WHAT CAN SOPHOMORES DO?

_____ Confirm your choice of major or seek help in changing to one that is better suited to your interests and abilities.

_____ Volunteer for jobs or positions in campus organizations that can help you acquire organizational, managerial, and leadership skills.

_____ Attend career days and job fairs to gather information about occupations that interest you.

_____ Take advantage of your campus career-planning resources, such as testing services, computerized career information systems, career library, and career counseling.

_____ Enroll in a career-planning course if you are still not certain about your major or career direction.

_____ Begin thinking of people whom you might ask to give you references, such as faculty or employers.

_____ Look for part-time or summer jobs that can provide work experiences to help you confirm your major and/or career choice.

_____ Begin to find out about co-op or internship possibilities for your junior or senior year.

_____ Continue to place in your "Job Search Information" folder the information you are collecting.

WHAT CAN JUNIORS DO?

_____ Conduct informational interviews in the career field you are considering.

_____ Begin to build a network of contacts in your field.

_____ Sign up for resume-writing workshops; take a workshop to practice interviewing techniques.

_____ Establish a credential file in your career services office; continue to collect letters of recommendation from faculty and others.

_____ Do serious research on possible employers and workplaces; collect lists available in your campus career planning and placement office or from other sources such as the library or the yellow pages.

_____ Seek internship or co-op placements for this year or your senior year.

_____ Update your resume.

_____ Find a summer job in a field related to your career goal.

_____ Improve your skills in the art of job searching on the Internet.

_____ Begin to look at the classified ads in the newspaper and clip ads for the ones that relate to your field of interest; put them in your "Job Search Information" folder along with other job descriptions you have been collecting.

WHAT CAN SENIORS DO?

_____ Register with your campus career services office.

_____ Take part in an internship or co-op experience, if available.

_____ Expand and refine your list of contacts.

_____ Examine what you have collected in your job search folder and make contacts with the persons or companies that have job possibilities.

_____ Update your resume; have it reproduced professionally.

_____ Create an electronic scannable resume in addition to your paper version.

_____ Invest in appropriate interviewing clothes.

_____ Update the references in your credential file in the career counseling office or those in your own file.

_____ Interview prospective employers through placement services.

_____ Learn to navigate the Web for on-line job searches.

_____ Contact off-campus work sites if needed.

_____ Use your co-op or internship experience to establish your work priorities.

_____ Consider job offers and weigh each on criteria you have established (opportunities to use your knowledge and skills, freedom to be creative, opportunities for promotion, salary and benefits package, relocation flexibility, lifestyle implications, etc.)

What steps do you need to take _now_ to move further along your career and job-search path (e.g., purchase a file folder, set up a personal file in your campus career services office, sign up for a resume-writing workshop)?

1. _____

2. _____

3. _____

4. _____

Writing a Resume

Your resume is one of the most important parts of your job search. A resume lists your accomplishments and experiences in a way that tells employers who you are and what you can contribute to their enterprise, whether it is in business, education, government, or another type of work environment.

Your resume is the first step in obtaining an interview. In the Internet age, many of the rules for resume writing are changing. Because most employers look at hundreds of resumes and screen them quickly, your resume must be impressive or it may end up in the wastebasket. Employers are often looking for key words such as *experience, success,* and *responsibility* and action verbs such as *coordinated, implemented, organized, performed,* and *achieved.* Key words are also important to employers as they scan resumes electronically. It takes careful thought and preparation to create a resume that presents you in the best possible light.

As we discussed earlier, your freshman year is the time to imagine how you will look on paper in the future. It is never too early to think about the skills, education, work experiences, and personal qualities that make you a unique person.

It is extremely useful early on to create an outline or general framework for your resume and fill in the sections as you progress through school. You then will have a running account of your experiences and accomplishments, some of which are important but easily forgotten. A sample resume worksheet is presented in Exercise 7.1.

EXERCISE 7.1 *Sample Resume Worksheet*

Name

Your name should stand out in bold capital letters, preferably centered on the page. You may want to put both your current and permanent addresses equally spaced under your name, if they're different. (This is especially important if your current address will change and you want to make certain an employer can reach you after a specific date.) Place your telephone number, including area code, under the address. If you have an e-mail address or FAX number, include it under your phone number.

Goals

Goals are what you project for yourself in the future: I want to work for a "Big Six" accounting firm; I want to work as a social worker in a hospital setting; I want to teach social studies in a high school. These phrases will be reworded later as career objectives—for example, "to obtain a position in public accounting" or "to use my skills and experiences as a social worker in a health care setting."

The goals and objectives you state on your resume must pertain directly to the type of job for which you are applying. This means that you may write several versions of your resume, depending on which objective or goal you use. Make your goals as specific as you can. Career objective statements can include the type of position you are seeking, the work environment you desire (e.g., industry, business, nonprofit, hospital), and the specific skills you bring to the position.

Put yourself in the place of a prospective employer. Do your goals realistically match the job or work environment? Your goals may change over time; this is a natural phenomenon. If you rewrite your goals, continue to state them in specific terms.

State a goal or career objective here:

_____

_____

_____

Qualifications Summary

If you have a great deal of work experience, you may want to insert a summary of it after your career objective statement.

Education

Your educational intent for now may be to obtain a specific degree (for example, "My goal is to obtain a bachelor of arts degree from Utopia University with a major in English and political science"; or "My goal is to obtain a bachelor of science degree in physical therapy"; or "I am working toward a master's degree in business administration"). Write below what your educational goal is now:

_____

_____

_____

In a resume, of course, you will list your degree(s) in a section about your educational background. Always arrange items in reverse chronological order if there is more than one (the most recent first). If you have received any honors, such as being on the Dean's list or other academic achievements, you may want to list them in this section. Include any special training you have received or credentials you have obtained. List relevant courses you took in college if they pertain to the job you seek. Your resume should include either an overall gradepoint average (GPA) or a GPA for courses in your major. (Be sure to specify which one.) You will have to decide whether to include this information. If not, be prepared to address this issue in an interview. A sample education section of a senior's resume might look like this:

> **EDUCATION**
>
> _Lincoln University,_ Ames, Minnesota. B.S. in Business Administration expected May 1, 2003, overall GPA: 3.0/4.0
>
> Extensive course work in consumer behavior, economics, technical writing, and computer science

Write below how you will list the items in your educational background (as you see them now):

_____

_____

_____

_____

_____

Work Experiences

You may want to place this section before the education section if your work experience is stronger. List your last place of employment with a description of your duties, followed by your other employment experience, in reverse chronological order. If you have acquired strong skills and limited work experience, you may want to consider the functional resume format, which highlights your abilities rather than emphasizing the sequence of your work experience. Experiences that show skills or functions in certain areas (e.g., organizational, managerial, interpersonal) can be grouped together. For example, under "organizational ability," you may want to describe your responsibilities as chairperson of the student-sponsored "Career Day" committee (e.g., coordinating committee, creating an advertising campaign, arranging the physical facilities). Another approach is to summarize your skills separately, after the education section.

Use action verbs in a resume, as they make your work experiences appear strong. Using action verbs brings your resume to life. For example, "supervised and trained five salespersons," or "responsible for ordering and managing stock," or "initiated and organized campuswide food drive." A list of sample action verbs follows.

accomplished	created	interpreted	produced
achieved	delegated	investigated	projected
adapted	demonstrated	launched	proposed
administered	developed	lectured	provided
analyzed	directed	led	qualified
applied	edited	maintained	researched
arranged	established	managed	revamped
assisted	executed	motivated	revised
budgeted	expedited	negotiated	scheduled
built	forecasted	observed	set up
chaired	formulated	operated	solved
changed	generated	organized	surveyed
communicated	guided	oversaw	trained
compiled	implemented	performed	transformed
conceived	initiated	persuaded	worked
conducted	instructed	planned	wrote

Employers focus on your activities and achievements and, through action verbs, you are conveying what you can do for them. Emphasize your strengths, accomplishments, abilities, past experiences, qualifications, and skills. You need to impress them with your ability to work well with others, learn quickly, and analyze and solve problems. Provide specific information so your qualities are measurable. For example, being promoted from cashier to assistant manager in a fast-food restaurant indicates responsibility and leadership qualities. Being elected to an office in a student organization can also show leadership qualities. List your present position in present tense; past positions in past tense.

List your work experiences to date in reverse chronological order (the most recent first):

_____

_____

_____

If you have experiences other than work that are relevant to your objective, you may want to add a section labeled "Other Experiences" or "Additional Experiences" here.

Additional Information

You may want to include on your resume pertinent information that does not fit into other sections, such as *Accomplishments* or *Honors,* that an employer might want to know. (For example, include (1) courses you have taken that directly relate to the job you are seeking, such as computer languages or technical writing; (2) study abroad; (3) if you have earned all or part of your college expenses; (4) membership in professional organizations; (5) being a published author; and (6) knowing a foreign language.) List some of your accomplishments below:

_____

_____

_____

Skill Identification

You may want to add a "skills" section to your resume, particularly if you're applying for a position for which *specific* skills are required. In Chapter Two you assessed your functional skills. Chapter Three emphasized many types of work skills as critical to the future workplace. If you have developed specific skills of which you want an employer to be aware, you may want to emphasize them on your resume. The action verbs used in relating work experiences reflect skills as well. Examples of skills might include:

initiated a project	compiled statistics
administered a program	wrote for publication
supervised others	researched in the library
developed software	negotiated a plan
budgeted expenses	resolved a conflict
coordinated a large event	investigated and resolved a problem
evaluated a program	

As stated in Chapter Two, we sometimes underestimate our ability to do certain tasks, even though we have the skills to accomplish them. Identifying skills in a specific section will inform a prospective employer of your marketable strengths.

When you have little work experience and are applying for an entry-level position, you may want to consider organizing your resume by skill areas rather than chronologically. This is called a *functional resume.* This format also may be useful to mature professionals who have a great deal of expertise or job experience in a field, individuals returning to the workforce after an extended absence, or career changers. A functional resume does not emphasize job titles or employers but, instead, focuses on skills and abilities. It has the advantage of emphasizing an individual's specific skills for a specific position.

Personal Data

Include personal information only if it is relevant to the job or if you are willing to relocate. Do not include height, weight, marital status, hobbies, or other information that is not relevant to the job or is illegal.

_____

_____

_____

References

Your references can make the difference between landing a job or not. *Be sure to obtain permission from anyone you are using as a reference!* Establish a file in your college's career services office, if that service is available. If not, keep your own file. You can ask employers, faculty, administrators, and other people who have come to know you personally to write letters of reference for your file. Request a letter of recommendation any time, as it sometimes is difficult in your senior year to obtain a recommendation from a faculty person with whom you worked as a sophomore or a junior. If you decide to go to graduate or professional school, faculty recommendations are especially important.

If you write "References upon request" in your resume, be prepared to provide them during an interview or as requested. If your college placement office maintains a service that will send your references at your request, you will want to list its name and address. Below, list the references you have already obtained. If you have not contacted references yet, write down the names of persons you want to contact.

_____

_____

_____

Using a worksheet such as this, you can maintain a running account of what you are accomplishing during your college career. Monitoring your progress can help you fill any gaps that may emerge as you analyze how your education, campus involvement, and work experiences are helping you reach your goals.

Final Touches

When you are ready to write a final version of your resume, you already will have completed the most difficult task of remembering and organizing the information you need. If you have not started this activity, it is never too late. Purchase a file folder, create a worksheet with the sections noted above, and begin to fill in the blanks with everything that comes into your mind, no matter how irrelevant it may seem at this time. Continue to record information in the folder as you accumulate school experiences, work in part-time or full-time summer jobs, or in any other situation in which you are acquiring relevant knowledge and skills. Do not put anything on your resume that you aren't prepared to elaborate on during an interview.

Avoid the common resume mistakes (see Figure 7.1). Check your final draft for poor grammar, misspelled words, and typographical errors. Don't be too sparse with certain information (giving only the bare essentials, understating what you accomplished in the past). On the other hand, don't write extended paragraphs or sentences that take too long to read. Keep the resume as short as possible (one page is enough, and never more than two for an entry-level position). A disorganized resume is hard to follow, so be certain it is easy to read, has plenty of "white space" (areas with no type or graphics), and looks professional.

One deadly error is to send a resume with information having no relationship to the organization or position. Creating more than one version of a resume gives you the opportunity to tailor the information to a specific job description. Revise goals, modify professional objectives, or rearrange work and volunteer activities to emphasize experience and skills that focus on the requirements for the specific position.

If you were an employer and received this resume, would you hire this person? What errors are evident? (The obvious errors are listed after the resume.)

DONALD WORD
1400 52nd Street
Oak Park, MA

Career Objective: To work in the business field

Education:

High School: Graduated from Finley High in 2000. Participated in sports.

Will graduate with a bachelors degree from Whitfield University hopefully in 2004 with a degree in biology

Work Experience:

Donney's Pizzaria, Oak Park, MA   2000

Worked parttime in sales and later as a cook.

McGill's Department Store, Oak Park, MA   2000 to present

I worked at McGill's department store as a clerk in sporting goods. In that job I sold sporting goods such as golf, baseball, and football equipment. I was also responsible for restocking shelves. This involved taking inventory dailey. I also waited on customers and answered their questions about our merchandize.

Other Work Experience:

Camp counselor at Bigfoot Camp, Maine—summers of 1999

Usher at Palace Theatre, Oak Park, MA—summer of 1998

Activities:

Play on intermural sports teams; dorm representative; Biology Club

Computer Skills: Familar with Word Perfect, E-mail and Internet search engines.

RESUME ERRORS:

No phone number, e-mail address, or zip code given

Incomplete "Objective"

Unattractive overall appearance; difficult to read

Work experiences not in chronological order; incomplete dates

Job description too wordy; more detail needed

Overuse of "I"

Misspelled words

Verb tenses not consistent (e.g., current job description should be in present tense)

No mention of references

Computerized resume packages are available. Your college career planning office may have a resume software package installed, or you may want to purchase one at a computer store. These packages can provide a quality, flexible resume development program. You can select the type of format you wish to use (chronological, skills, functional) and indicate the typestyle and any graphics you desire. Resume programs ask specific questions relating to career objectives, work experience, and education. Your resume will be on a disk so you can update it easily.

Video Resumes

A relatively new approach to resume dissemination, although it is somewhat costly, is the video resume. Some job-search firms are asking their clients to talk about themselves on a 5- to 10-minute video. Videos offer an added dimension to the hiring process, because employers can screen prospects for an interview based on how they present themselves on the video. Some employers like video resumes because they save the company time, money, and even travel. Some employers may not care for the video resume, so you will have to determine their attitude toward this technique before sending one. If you do decide to send a video resume, make sure it is a professional product.

Electronic Resumes

An important approach is the electronic resume. Placing your resume on the Internet offers another avenue for selling yourself in a competitive market. The three basic types of electronic resume submission are e-mail, on-line, and newsgroups.

E-mail is the most common method for electronically submitting a resume. Some employers require you to send your resume via this method. They will assume you have basic computer skills and are Web-literate. When using a newsgroup, a resume may be loaded the same way as through e-mail.

Scannable Resumes

Employers who receive large numbers of resumes are now using computers to store them. The computer scans keywords relating to the posted positions and places them in the appropriate file. Resumes collected in this way must be adjusted so they are readable. It is advisable to add a section containing the keywords from your resume that are specifically relevant to the position for which you are applying so the computer will select it during a search. These keywords can include skills (e.g., specific computer skills), work experiences (e.g., research), or educational information (e.g., Finance major). Many resume-scanning systems recognize nouns as opposed to verbs.

For the scannable format, resumes have to be simplified. For example, do not use graphics, highlighting, different fonts, underlining, parentheses, asterisks, or italics. Columns also will confuse the computer. No line of text should be longer than 65 characters. You may want to send a copy of your regular resume along with a scannable version, as some employers still prefer the printed variety. Always include a cover letter.

Because software programs vary, your resume as an e-mail attachment may not be compatible with that of the organization to which you are sending it. Therefore, make it part of your e-mail message, not an attachment. Or save your document as a generic ASCII (text only) file. In addition to sending your resume by e-mail, mail a printed copy and cover letter. Using e-mail will make a quick impression, but following up with a more traditional approach will ensure that the employer receives it. As with traditional resumes, observe the rules of concise, well-prepared documents.

An on-line resume is a Web document available to any employer. An advantage of an on-line service is that it can easily be posted and submitted to appropriate areas. On-line resumes are read by employers in computer-related industries, and increasingly by employers in many types of businesses (such as retail, marketing, finance, and education), and nonprofit organizations.

Examples of websites that include resume postings and/or job listings are

www.careermosaic.com

www.att.com/college

www.careerpath.com

www.espan.com

Preparing for your future now is the key to an effective job-search campaign. Although there are no set rules for writing a resume, your intent is to make the most favorable impression possible. Don't be modest; this is the time to emphasize your strengths. Use the blank resume worksheet in Exercise 7.2 to start collecting this information if you have not already done so.

Appearance

How your resume looks is as important as its content. Arrange the information so it appears well-organized and professional. If you do not have access to a computer and an excellent printer, consider using those available at quick-print shops. With a computer you can prepare several versions and make changes quickly. You also can store a general cover letter and revise it as needed to include specific, personalized information about each prospective employer. A poorly prepared resume or cover letter reflects poor work habits.

Ask at least one person to proofread your resume before sending it. Poor grammar, misspellings, and other errors are unacceptable. Also, a resume that is too fancy can distract from the central message. Avoid colored paper or paper that does not duplicate clearly, as an employer may copy your resume many times. It is especially important to keep your resume simple when faxing or sending it electronically. Underlining, bullets, and small type, as examples, may not be clearly reproduced.

Figures 7.2–7.7 are some examples of how to organize and present material. Figure 7.2 is an improved version of the resume in Figure 7.1. The others are examples of chronological, functional and skills styles of resumes, as well as a resume for a summer job.

Job Searching on the Internet

The Internet offers vast resources for jobhunters. Aspects of the Internet useful for this task are the World Wide Web, Telnet, Gopher, newsgroups, mailing lists appearing in advertisements and magazine and newspaper articles, and e-mail for making contact with prospective employers. Cyber-recruiting is increasing as more employers are turning to the Web. This means that as a job-seeker, you will need to learn the techniques for using this medium.

On-line resources such as CompuServe, America Online, and Prodigy offer many career-related services, including resume posting and job openings. One example is the Online Career Center (www.occ.com). Contact your campus career office to post your resume on its system.

EXERCISE 7.2 *Resume worksheet*

MY PERSONAL GOALS (CAREER OBJECTIVES)

_____

_____

_____

_____

_____

_____

_____

EDUCATION

_____

_____

_____

_____

_____

_____

_____

_____

WORK EXPERIENCES/SKILLS ACQUIRED

_____

_____

_____

_____

_____

_____

_____

CAMPUS ACTIVITIES

_____

_____

_____

_____

_____

_____

_____

VOLUNTEER

_____
_____
_____
_____
_____
_____

RELEVANT COURSE WORK

_____
_____
_____
_____
_____
_____

HONORS

_____
_____
_____
_____
_____

OTHER KNOWLEDGE/TALENTS/SKILLS

_____
_____
_____
_____
_____

REFERENCES

_____
_____
_____
_____
_____
_____

FIGURE 7.2 *Improved resume for Donald Word.*

Donald Word

1400 52nd Street
Oak Park, MA 12345

(209) 721-4567
dword@whitfield.edu

OBJECTIVE

Seeking a sales or marketing internship with a pharmaceutical company

EDUCATION

Whitfield University, Waverly, MA
Bachelor of Science, Biology, May, 2004
GPA: 3.20
Self-financing 80% of college expenses

EXPERIENCE

McGill's Department Store, Oak Park, MA
Clerk, December, 2000 – present
- Sell sporting goods, such as golf, soccer, baseball, and football equipment
- Respond to customers' questions about pricing and selection
- Inventory equipment daily and stock shelves
- Receive customer payments and balance cash drawer daily

Donney's Pizzeria, Oak Park, MA
Cook, May – August, 2000
- Received phone orders from customers, accurately recorded them and gave to cooks
- Promoted to cook after six weeks

Bigfoot Camp, Shady Hill, ME
Camp Counselor, Summer, 1999
- Assisted with activities for a group of six 10-year-old boys
- Planned weekly group meeting
- Planned weekly team activity with my group

Palace Theater, Oak Park, MA
Usher, Summer, 1998
- Received tickets from customers and directed to theaters
- Assisted disabled customers in getting to their theater
- Cleaned theaters after each showing

ACTIVITIES

- Biology Club
- Residence Hall floor representative
- Whitfield University intramural basketball and baseball

COMPUTER SKILLS

Word, e-mail, and Internet search engines

REFERENCES

Available on request.

DENNIS DOE

30 Raspberry Road, Columbus, Ohio 43213
614-924-3456 • doe.9@liv.edu

Professional Objective

To obtain a position as an account executive in the public relations field

Key Word Summary

Leadership, internship, marketing

Education

Bachelor of Science, Lincoln University, Columbus, Ohio

Expected June 2003; Business Administration

Major in marketing, minor in English; extensive course work in consumer behavior, economics, technical writing, computer science, GPA 3.2/4.0

Earning 75 percent of college expenses.

Work Experience

Glass Public Relations Company, Columbus, Ohio, Intern   6/01 to present

Assist with drafting copy for, designing, and proofreading public relations materials such as ad campaigns, brochures, and annual reports; use computer graphics programming, including Harvard Graphics.

Lincoln University Trumpet, Columbus, Ohio, Student Reporter   9/98 to 6/01

Wrote humor column on students' perspectives of campus life. Covered various academic departments; interviewed faculty from Humanities department on a regular basis; attended student organization meetings, and wrote summaries of student activities.

Hewlett Bookstore, Suncity, Ohio, Assistant to Manager   6/96 to 9/98

Responsible for stocking inventory for large bookstore; refined system for ordering and shelving stock; worked with promotional material; supervised three part-time workers.

Activities

Elected president of Alpha Kappa Phi business honorary; served on Dean's student advisory council, School of Business; member, National Business Students Association; co-chaired annual campuswide career fair.

Additional Skills

Computer skills   familiar with Lotus 1-2-3, Adobe Pagemaker (IBM), Macintosh, Harvard Graphics, Internet applications: knowledge of html, E-mail, WWW, Microsoft Office

Languages   fluent in French

References

References are attached.

FIGURE 7.4 *Functional resume.*

DENNIS DOE

30 Raspberry Road   614-924-3456
Columbus, Ohio 43213   doe.9@liv.edu

PROFESSIONAL OBJECTIVE
To obtain a position as an account executive in the public relations field

KEY WORD SUMMARY
Leadership, internship, marketing

EDUCATION
Bachelor of Science, Lincoln University, Columbus, Ohio
  Expected, June 2003; business administration
  Major in marketing, minor in English; extensive coursework in consumer behavior, economics, technical writing, computer science, GPA 3.2/4.0
  Earned 75 percent of college expenses.

SKILLS
Writing
- Assisted with drafting copy and proofreading of public relations materials during internship with Glass Public Relations Company.
- Reporter for student newspaper; wrote articles about academic departments and student organizations.
- Wrote weekly humor column on students' perspectives on campus life for college newspaper.

Organizational
- Organized campuswide Career Day; contacted over 100 employers to participate; arranged special workshops as part of overall program.
- Responsible for stocking inventory for Hewlett Bookstore.
- Refined system for ordering and shelving stock.
- Supervised staff of three part-time workers.
- Worked with promotional material under manager's supervision.

Leadership
- Elected president of business honorary; acted as liaison with alumni in many types of businesses.
- Coordinated activities of 10-member committee for campuswide Career Day.
- Served on Dean's student advisory council.

EMPLOYMENT HISTORY
Glass Public Relations Company, Columbus, Ohio
  June 2001 to present
Hewlett Bookstore, Suncity, Ohio
  June 1997 to September 1999

ADDITIONAL SKILLS
- Computer skills—familiar with Lotus 1-2-3, Adobe Pagemaker, Macintosh, Harvard Graphics, Microsoft Office
- Internet applications: knowledge of HTML, e-mail, WWW
- Languages—fluent in French

REFERENCES
References available upon request

MARLENE BROOK

current address:
444 Stone Place
Sheetrock, CA 93076
714-555-1898
FAX: 714-555-1492

permanent address:
2234 Ames Way
Amherst, CA 93779
213-555-4549

OBJECTIVE

To obtain a position in an international company where I can use my proven sales skills and fluency in French

EDUCATION

Sheetrock College, Sheetrock, CA
Bachelor of Arts, history major,
French minor
May 2002, GPA 3.35

PROFESSIONAL EXPERIENCE

6/01–present

Third National Bank, Sheetrock, CA
Accounts Receivable Clerk
- Post deposit transactions
- Work with automated account system

6/98–6/01

Packard's Restaurant, Bryant, CA
Assistant Manager
- Responsible for operations of family restaurant's morning shift
- Directed work of four employees
- Increased sales through vigorous advertising campaign
- Started as waitress

6/89–6/98

Missus Clothes Horse, Bryant, CA
Salesperson
- Sold women's clothing in specialty shop
- Exceeded sales quota by 50 percent

ACTIVITIES

International Students Organization:
volunteer mentor; assisted with orientation for new international students;
Union Board; coordinated student artwork program

ADDITIONAL INFORMATION

Computer training in Lotus, Microsoft Office
Study Abroad Program: studied in Paris junior year of high school;
extensive travel in Europe; fluent in French
Earned 100 percent of college expenses

REFERENCES

Available upon request.

FIGURE 7.6   *Skills resume.*

MARY L. JONESFIELD
53 Oak Street, Apt. 203, Newport, Louisiana 70790   (232) 777-1234   M.Jonesfield@netlink.com

OBJECTIVE   To obtain an entry-level management position in retailing

SKILLS
- Gained expertise in retail sales
- Assisted in buying merchandise
- Arranged floor displays
- Resolved customer problems
- Organized and maintained inventories

EDUCATION   Cranston College, Evans, Louisiana
B.A. in Communications, June 1994
Coursework emphasized organizational communications
Took courses in marketing, management, and consumer behavior

HONORS   Dean's List; Academic Scholarship

ACTIVITIES   Residence Hall Advisor; elected representative to Undergraduate Student Government (two terms); president of Spanish Club

WORK EXPERIENCE

June 1998 to present

Gordon's Department Store, Bland, Louisiana
Salesperson
- Sell clothing in children's department
- Learned extensive inventory
- Developed sales techniques
- Increased sales by 25 percent in six months

August 1996 to July 1998

R. J. Imports, Newport, Louisiana
Salesperson
- Sold a variety of imported products, including bric-a-brac and clothing
- Monitored and organized current stock
- Started as stock person; promoted to sales after three months

ADDITIONAL INFORMATION   Computer training in QuatroPro, Quicken, Lotus 1-2-3
Competent in word processing, especially Microsoft Word
Willing to travel or relocate

REFERENCES   Available upon request.

Steven R. Gall

Box 104, Appleton Hall, Conrad College, Micro, TN 38456   gall.42@aol.com   (595) 556-9876

JOB OBJECTIVE

To obtain an internship or summer employment in an art gallery or museum that will allow me to use my experience in art and my education in art history.

EDUCATION

Conrad College, 2002 to present
Bachelor of Arts, 2003
GPA 3.0/4.0, art history major

WORK EXPERIENCE

Volunteer, Sojourn Museum   *Summer 2002*
Sojourn, TN
- Assisted in preparing three exhibits

Camp Counselor, Art Appreciation Camp   *Summer 2001*
Sunset, TN
- Counselor for children ages 7–10
- Developed and led art programs for small groups of children
- Assisted with waterfront activities

Volunteer, Francisco Gallery   *6/96 to 6/98*
Sojourn, TN
- Helped arrange exhibits
- Served as docent for special showings with different customers including children and seniors
- Unpacked and prepared art materials for shipping

COMPUTER SKILLS

- Microsoft Office
- Internet applications: E-mail, WWW

REFERENCES

Furnished upon request

Writing a Cover Letter

Along with your resume, you should include a cover letter addressed to the specific person you want to contact. If you are not sure of the person to whom it should be sent, call the company for the appropriate contact. Ask for the correct spelling of the name and the person's title and address. A cover letter should be brief, but you may want to include additional information not on your resume and emphasize experience specific to the job for which you are applying.

In the first paragraph, briefly indicate how you learned of the position and why you are interested in it. If you are responding to a job posting or ad, state the position title, where you saw the posting, and the date it was posted. If you were referred by an individual, state his or her name and title. In two or three additional paragraphs, review your relevant strengths and qualifications as they relate to this specific position. Do not repeat everything already included in your resume; cover letters should be brief and to the point.

In a closing paragraph, indicate that you are available for an interview at the addressee's convenience. Always include a current phone number where you can be reached. (It is helpful to have an answering machine with a professional outgoing message so a prospective employer can leave a message if you are not home.)

Your cover letter may be the hook that gets someone to read your resume. Figures 7.8, 7.9, and 7.10 are examples of cover letters. If you do not receive a response within two weeks of sending your resume and cover letter, telephone the person to verify that it was received and inquire about your status.

You should be acquiring information and skills throughout your college years. Learning to write a resume is one of the most basic skills in this process. First-year students benefit from seeing themselves on paper; it helps set goals, ascertain weaknesses, and use time and opportunities in college to acquire skills and experiences vital to becoming a strong job candidate. Upper-level students can refine to a prospective employer how they will appear on paper. As you continually update your resume, include the positive changes and experiences you have gained that not only will enhance your perspective of your marketability but also will put you ahead of the game when it's time to find a job.

We have seen how you can reflect a positive, confident attitude through a well-organized resume and a good cover letter. Preparing for the job search also requires skills to learn how to make direct contact with prospective employers. Chapter Eight covers this important phase of the job-search process.

30 Raspberry Road
Columbus, Ohio 43213
March 1, 2001

Ruth Redman, Director
Clearer Images, Inc.
202 Parkway Drive
Columbus, Ohio 43258

Dear Ms. Redman:

By way of this letter and attached resume, I am writing to apply for the position of copywriter with Clearer Images, Inc., which I learned about through Lincoln University's College of Business career services office. Your work at Clearer Images is innovative, and your brochures and annual reports are most impressive.

Currently I am completing coursework for my bachelor's degree in marketing. As you can see from my enclosed resume, I have a range of skills and talents that match well the job requirements you describe. I gained hands-on experience in my work as an intern with the Glass Public Relations Company—preparing copy, layout formats, and computer graphics programming.

In addition, I was a staff reporter for Lincoln University's campus publication, *Trumpet,* during my sophomore year and wrote a weekly humor column about student life. Enclosed are two clips for your review. I also covered events for several academic departments and enjoyed interviewing faculty members. My areas of expertise and interest include marketing, economics, and languages.

I am eager to learn more about the copywriter position at Clearer Images, Inc. I will call you during the week of March 15 to set up an appointment that is convenient for you. If you wish to contact me, please call 614-924-3456 or contact me by e-mail: doe.9@liv.edu. Thank you for your consideration.

Sincerely,

Dennis Doe

Dennis Doe

Enclosures

FIGURE 7.9   *Cover letter #2.*

2220 Smith Hall
18 S. 11th Avenue
Columbus, Ohio 43210
May 3, 2002

Aldo Smythe
Director of Human Resources
Blank Management Systems
88 Stretch Drive
Cleveland, Ohio 40404

Dear Mr. Smythe:

In response to the job posting for an accountant, which I reviewed at Ohio State's College of Business career services office, I am enclosing my resume. As you can see, I have worked in a variety of business settings and was fortunate to have been selected for a summer management-training internship at Acme, Inc., in 1996. In addition, my accounting degree has prepared me well for the specific tasks outlined in your job description, and I believe I would make a positive contribution to your company.

Being from the Cleveland area, I am familiar with your company's fine reputation and I am aware of the emphasis your firm places on strong managers and on hiring people with leadership skills. I would like to discuss with you in person what I can contribute to Blank Management Systems. Next week I will be in Cleveland and will telephone you to see if we can schedule an appointment to discuss my qualifications. This week I can be reached at (614) 292-0000. Thank you for your consideration.

Sincerely,

Jane Denny

Jane Denny

Enclosure

113 South Street
Fortner, Idaho 35789
April 20, 2001

Mr. Alexander Q. Paul, Curator
Denver Historical Museum
210 High Street
Denver, CO 84040

Dear Mr. Paul:

Through this letter and attached resume, I am applying for a position with the Denver Historical Museum. I will receive the bachelor's degree in history and anthropology in June. The excellent education I received in these areas is supported by hands-on work I have done in several museums. My knowledge, experience, and enthusiasm would be an asset to your enterprise.

As my resume indicates, I have worked in museums both as an employee and a volunteer. I have assisted curators with research, set up exhibits, prepared objects for shipment, and acted as tour guide for many types of groups, including groups of children and senior citizens. At the Museum of History in Boise, I helped create exhibits about Western American Indian tribes that displayed many priceless artifacts.

Perhaps my most challenging experience was to participate in a dig with Professor Don Jones in southern Idaho, where American Indian artifacts have been discovered. Working on this dig allowed me to put my knowledge of history and anthropology to practical use and gave me a sense of the natural settings in which such artifacts should be displayed.

I look forward to talking with you in detail about how my education and work experience would be an asset to the Denver Historical Museum. I will call you next week to request an appointment. In the meantime, I can be reached at 315-333-4040, or by e-mail at Parker_Rudd@UI.edu. Thank you for your consideration.

Sincerely,

Parker T. Rudd

Parker T. Rudd

Enclosure

CHOICE AND COMMITMENT As Jed checked the items in Chapter Seven on what he should be doing as a first-year student, he realized that he needed to be working on all of them, especially those related to academic work. To start taking some action toward his goal of teaching, he decided to apply for a summer job at his home city's recreation department to gain experience in that area. To do this, he had to write a resume and learn how to interview. He used the resume computer program in the campus' career services office and showed a rough draft to his career course instructor. His teacher offered some changes and additions and suggested that Jed show the next draft to an expert in the career services office. After a few more changes suggested by the resume expert, Jed was confident that he had created a clear and concise picture of his skills and experiences for the recreation job.

At Christmas break Jed filled out an application and left his resume and a cover letter with the recreation department. As a back-up, he applied at the swimming pool where he had been a lifeguard the previous two summers. He decided that at spring break he would apply for a summer sales job at a sporting goods store near his home. He also decided to volunteer as a base-ball coach for a Little League team. Now that he had a direction and goal, he felt very good about the decisions he was making to carry out those goals.

Maria had put together a resume many years ago when she entered her first job out of high school, but she has updated it only sporadically. When she compared her resume worksheet to those of some of the other students in the class, she realized that she had many skills and work experiences that the younger students did not. She realized that the computer skills she has been developing over the years are substantial and should be emphasized on her resume.

An older student in the class told Maria about the help he had received from a counselor in the career services office on her campus, and Maria decided to take her final version there for a professional opinion. Although Maria is not job-hunting at this time, it occurs to her that she may be able to find a better paying position in another company to alleviate her financial situation. She plans to discuss with her present supervisor a possible promotion within the company. This will give her the motivation to update her resume to reflect her new abilities and goals.

CHAPTER 7 *Summary Checklist*

What I have learned

_____ I have learned the basic components of an effective resume and gathered relevant information about myself in each of these areas.

_____ I have written a resume emphasizing my strengths and, through its appearance and format, portraying me in the best possible light.

———— I now recognize areas of my resume that are weak and have established a plan to acquire the skills and experiences needed to make me an outstanding job candidate.

———— I have the skills to submit an electronic resume and can conduct a job search on the Internet.

———— I understand the importance of a cover letter, its purpose, and what it should include.

How I can use it

I can write an impressive resume and feel confident that an employer will want to interview me after reading it.

Eight

Am I the Best Candidate?

JOB LEADS AND THE JOB INTERVIEW

Generating Job Leads

In the preceding chapters you reviewed and refined your personal perspectives of "career," examined your personal characteristics and how they might be compatible with certain career fields, experienced the decision-making process, and learned about the future work world. In addition, you learned how to present yourself in the best possible light using different types of resumes. The next step is to present yourself to a prospective employer as an applicant for a specific job. If you already hold a job or have worked part-time, you probably have been interviewed. This chapter provides information about the interviewing process and its part in ensuring a successful outcome.

Only one-fourth of job openings are advertised in the classified ads. You will need to tap the "hidden market" and pursue as many different sources of information as possible. Start by making a list of everyone you know in your field of interest. Contacting these individuals will not always lead to a possible job opening, but if you get their support and endorsement, you may gain an edge over another applicant.

The Internet has changed dramatically how many workers now apply for jobs. More than 60 percent of employers post jobs electronically, and some are adding on-line recruiting. Not learning to use this medium in your job search might place you at a disadvantage. As indicated in Chapter Seven, many websites include resume postings and job listings. This is not to discount the use of the traditional job search methods that follow but it is wise to use all the resources available in your job search. The source descriptions discussed next will help you formulate a plan for generating contacts.

Informational Interviewing

If you previously have interviewed people in careers that interest you (see Chapter Three), you probably have a wealth of valuable information that cannot be gleaned from books or other literature on careers. If you have not interviewed anyone, you may want to consider doing so now, for practice. It will allow you to practice your interviewing skills and thereby gain insights into the person's daily tasks, background and experience, personal reflections on the work, information about promotions and other opportunities for advancement, how the career choice has affected the person's lifestyle, and recommended preparations.

Before contacting a prospective interviewee, you must be well-prepared. Call the person with whom you wish to speak at the worksite. People you contact often will be referrals from friends, family, faculty, or your career-planning office. The yellow pages of the phone book offer additional possible sources and ideas. When you call for an interview appointment, emphasize that you are seeking *information,* not applying for a job. Suggest a specific time limit for the interview—for instance, 20 to 30 minutes.

Networking

Informational interviews are the first step in creating a network of people to contact at various times in your job search. You will want to add to your network in other ways as well. When you talk with friends, family, faculty members, past employers, and others, ask if they can provide names of any prospective employers. If you ask every individual you talk with for one or two possible "leads," in time your networking efforts likely will lead to an actual job interview. Be sure to record carefully in a notebook the name of any referral, as well as his or her title, address, and phone number, and keep track of who referred you to that individual.

As in informational interviewing, careful preparation is essential before actually making the contact. Be certain you are clear about why this person's job is relevant to your own job search before writing a letter or phoning for an appointment. After you have made the contact, write the result in your notebook.

Newspapers

If you started a job-search file earlier, find the clippings from the "help wanted" section of newspapers in the city where you want to work. Study the classified ads in the newspapers regularly to keep abreast of the market. Again, most jobs are not listed in newspapers. The newspaper is only one of many resources. Following up on a newspaper ad, however, can provide the type of experience you need to sharpen your cover letters and, sometimes, to use your interviewing skills.

Employment Services

Entry-level jobs occasionally are listed with employment agencies, which receive a commission on every position they fill. Interviewing for a job through an employment service is good practice for determining the effectiveness of your resume and interviewing skills. Experienced workers may want to contact a "headhunter," a person who works for an employment service to place people in high-level positions.

If you are required to sign an agreement with an employment service, be certain that you understand the terms of the contract. Sometimes the employer pays the commission. Other contracts require the employee to pay a fee.

Job Fairs

Your school may offer a job fair, to which prospective employers are invited to share information about their company or services with students in a large, informal setting. Students have the opportunity to peruse different companies by walking from table to table, picking up printed information, and talking personally with company representatives who can explain the type of work they do, the jobs they have open, and the background, training, and personal attributes they seek in prospective employees.

Job fairs are excellent vehicles for gathering information and asking questions in an informal setting. Even though you may be only a first- or second-year student, you can learn a great deal by attending job fairs. As an upper-level student, you can easily and quickly expand your contacts and learn about new employment possibilities.

Friends and Family

Many people find jobs through personal contacts gleaned from family, friends, or acquaintances. These leads are fruitful because the employer is more apt to view you positively on the basis of a good recommendation from a mutual contact than from a "cold call" or "blind resume." When using this type of referral, your goal is to get an interview. When you do, it is up to you to make a strong case for why you are the best person for the job.

Direct Contacts

Targeting specific types of employers can be a productive approach. You can study the type of work they perform and determine if it matches your own interests and skills. Send a resume with a cover letter to a *specific individual,* indicating why you would like to meet with that person. Then follow up with a phone call. Often your letter will be prescreened, so the employer may not see it. Be persistent in your effort. When you finally reach the person, be prepared to impress the individual with your knowledge of the company and how your background, training, and experience would make you an asset to the organization. The idea here is to persuade the potential employer to meet with you. Use the suggestions in the "interviewing" section of this chapter whenever you make personal contacts.

Although people are busy, they often enjoy discussing their job with students or others who are in the process of exploring career possibilities. Share the information you have already obtained about their field from your research, and ask if it is accurate from their perspective. You also may want to ask your interviewees for names of other people in similar positions so you may *extend your informational interviewing network.*

Stick to the time you have allotted. Thank the interviewees for their insights and follow up with a thank-you letter. Write down the interviewee's name, title, place of employment, and the important facts you obtained. File this information in your job-search folder. Although these interviews are not the same as interviewing for a "real" job, the practice and contacts you make can be critical factors in your job search later.

Career Mentors

Many successful workers have been helped by someone who has given them guidance—a mentor who helped them to learn important things about their work environment and career. A mentor is an experienced person who has "been there" and is willing to help a new associate. Mentors can give advice and personal support. They can help you develop knowledge and skills that are essential for you to become integrated into a new work environment and better understand what the job requires. You may already have a mentor in another part of your life (e.g., school, community activity). That person also may be an excellent source of information for possible networking contacts or even job prospects.

Job Interviewing

It is helpful to think of interviewing in three stages: *preparing* for the interview, how to conduct yourself *during* the interview, and what to do *after* the interview. When direct contact, resumes, and cover letters result in an interview, how you prepare is vital. Most screening interviews last about 30 minutes, and the first five minutes usually set the tone. First impressions are important.

Preparing for the Interview

Any information you have learned about the company and other prospective places of employment will tell the interviewees you are serious about working there. Most companies publish information about their purpose, priorities, and financial situation, as well as other pertinent facts. You can obtain this information from annual reports, product information brochures, and library resources such as business periodicals and newspapers. This type of information also is available at your career planning and placement office or directly from the company. Studying the information can help you prepare relevant questions, focus on employers' needs, and understand how you can contribute to their mission. Anxiety about interviews is natural, but you will be more relaxed and confident if you feel well-prepared.

Many career planning and placement offices offer workshops on how to interview. Some even provide the opportunity for you to videotape a mock interview with a professional employer, who then gives feedback on your performance. Or you can organize mock interviews with your friends and family. Practice builds interviewing skills and teaches you habits to avoid, such as not making eye contact and talking too much. If you are able to arrange a mock interview with an employer, ask questions to elicit feedback, such as the following:

What was your first impression of me?

What was your impression of my overall appearance? Physical and nonverbal mannerisms? Tone and speed of speech?

How would you rate my listening skills?

How clear was I in expressing my personal goals and objectives?

How would you rate the discussion of my educational and work experiences?

What was my level of knowledge of the organization and the position I was applying for?

How did I respond to the substance of your questions?

Did I ask relevant and thoughtful questions as the interview progressed?

What was your impression of my level of enthusiasm and interest in the position?

Would you hire me? Why or why not?

During the Interview

You want to convey an image of confidence throughout the interview. If you have prepared carefully, you probably will relax once it is under way and realize you are able to ask and answer questions succinctly and comfortably. Try to analyze the interviewer's style, and respond in the same manner. Behave formally if the interviewer sets a formal tone. If the interviewer asks questions quickly and moves on to the next, respond similarly.

Interviewers are quick to pick up on nonverbal mannerisms that indicate nervousness (e.g., looking around the room, nervously fingering your pen). Make good eye contact, listen intently, and ask and answer questions thoughtfully. Be well-prepared, but don't practice so much that you sound "canned." Be spontaneous and honest. An honest self-evaluation will impress an interviewer. Be prepared to talk about your strengths as well as your weaknesses. You can turn a shortcoming into a positive statement:

> "One of my weaknesses is being a perfectionist. I'm a diligent worker, but I'm getting better at understanding that everything doesn't have to be perfect."

Interviewers often ask similar basic questions. Anticipating these questions gives you a chance to formulate your answers and practice them in mock interview sessions. Other questions may depend on the type of position or the interviewer's style. Sample questions an interviewer might ask include:

Tell me about yourself.

Why do you think you are suited for this particular position?

Have you worked in this field before?

Do you understand what this job entails? (A discussion of the job can lead to observations about your abilities, experience, attitudes, etc.)

What are your greatest strengths? What are your greatest weaknesses?

Name two or three accomplishments that have given you the most satisfaction.

How do you perform under pressure?

Do you have any outside activities that would make it impossible to work evenings or weekends as required by this position?

What was your previous place of employment, and who were your supervisors, peers, or trainers?

How many hours a week do you think someone should devote to a job?

How did you finance your college education?

From what I have told you about this company, do you think you would like working here? Why?

Do you have any other information about yourself that would help me make a decision about filling this job?

One frequently asked question is, "Tell me about yourself." You might respond briefly by describing the personal qualities that are relevant to the position for which you are interviewing. Describe your educational background, related work experience, and some of your personal strengths. For example:

> "I will graduate in June with a degree in communications. I was president of the communications club and was elected to our college's administrative council. I interned twice with a local public relations firm and was invited to work part-time as a result of that experience. I'm a hard worker and well organized. I'm an excellent writer and have been told I have creative ways of approaching different problems."

Another common question is, "Why do you want this job?" This is a good time to reiterate your goals, strengths, special qualities, and how they relate to the job for which you are interviewing.

"My goal is to obtain a position where I can use my interests and talents in writing and marketing. Your position is very appealing because it appears to offer the type of work I love and have prepared for. My internship experiences confirmed my interest in public relations, and I think I can contribute a great deal to your organization."

Although you should wait for the interviewer to bring up the question of salary, you should be prepared for the question, "What salary do you expect?" You will already have studied the salary range for the job for which you are applying—or a specific salary may have been designated for the job. Your knowledge about the salary will show the interviewer you have done your homework. If you are not certain, ask for more details before responding.

Employers sometimes are more influenced by negative information than positive information. Even though you are presenting yourself in your most favorable light, your interviewers often give more weight to unfavorable information or impressions to narrow down the field. Even a small negative may shift an interviewer's impression—for example, saying you are never available to work overtime.

You also should be prepared to ask questions of your own based on the information you have gathered. Writing them down ahead of time will help you organize your thoughts. You might ask your interviewer about other students from your school who are employed by the company and how they have advanced. Listen for value-laden statements by the interviewer, such as those concerning expectations about work-time commitment. Ask questions about the company policies that are important to you. Try to determine if your work values match those of the company's culture.

Employers may use one of several types of interviews, including the traditional question-and-answer session, in which an interviewer and interviewee use a *structured* format. The *unstructured* style is similar to a conversation. A more recent type is the *targeted* approach, in which the questions asked are used to measure the interviewee's potential in critical areas such as problem solving and leadership. The interviewee is asked to cite examples of past performance in designated areas.

An example is the STAR Technique. STAR stands for situation, tasks, actions, and results. Interviewees are asked to describe a project, problem, or *situation* in which they have been involved. They are asked to describe the major *tasks* in that situation, the *actions* they took and the *results* (outcomes). Examples of target questions might be: "Describe a situation where you had to talk to an individual or group causing a problem" or "Tell me about the most difficult decision you've ever had to make." Your answers should be based on actual past or current situations. Your focus should be on reporting factual information, not hypothetical situations. Responses to these types of questions require preparation, so think through (*before* the interview) possible situations that include all the components of a complete STAR.

Appearance

Making a good impression includes physical appearance as well as how you ask and respond to questions. How you dress sometimes depends on the type of job you are seeking. When you present an attractive appearance, the interviewer will know you are aware of the importance of conveying a professional image. Find out how people dress in the work environment where you are interviewing. A safe approach is to wear conservative, contemporary, but comfortable clothes for any interview, even if the employees are allowed to wear jeans. Use jewelry and fragrance in moderation. In any event, an interviewer often will measure your seriousness and maturity by your appearance.

Etiquette

Although old-fashioned manners often are taken for granted, some job seekers need a refresher course. It is always proper for men and women alike to stand to shake hands when being greeted, for example. Table manners at a business lunch can communicate volumes about a candidate. In the Internet age, etiquette in the job-search process is changing constantly. Questions about high-tech etiquette are still being asked, such as how to use e-mail and voice mail. When in doubt, use common sense. A traditional approach is probably best when no clear rule exists.

After the Interview

You should write a follow-up thank-you letter to the interviewer to reiterate your interest in the position. A phone call also might be valuable. Reflect on the interview and write down areas in which you did well and those in which you need to improve. Be realistic in your evaluation of the outcomes of the interview.

Cyber-Interviews

Software is now available by which to interview job applicants. Prospective employees are asked a series of questions about their career goals and work history. Applicants' responses are rated, and those with the highest ratings are invited for a personal interview. A variation of this method is a telephone call in which the applicant answers questions on a push-button phone.

Legal and Illegal Questions

The Fair Employment Practices Act designates certain hiring practices as illegal. These include procedures and questions related to interviewing. Employers are not allowed to inquire about nationality, religious affiliation, age, race, marital status, pregnancy, disabilities, arrest records, or drug or alcohol addiction. If you think this information is relevant to the position, however, you can volunteer the information.

If you think you have been asked an illegal question, you may want to answer it with another question (e.g., "In what way is this related to this position?"). Or if the question is an obvious violation, you need to be assertive and give your reason for not answering. Violations should be reported to the director of your campus placement office if the interview took place under its auspices, so appropriate action may be taken. *How* questions are asked is also important. Here are examples of legal and illegal interview questions:

ILLEGAL	LEGAL
(Inquiries into a foreign address that would indicate national origin)	What is your current address, and how long have you lived there?
Are there certain religious holidays you will not be working?	Are you willing to work a required schedule?
Have you ever been arrested?	Have you ever been arrested for or convicted of anything related to the qualifications for this job?
What is your native language?	Do you speak and/or write any other languages fluently?

Will you provide names, ages, addresses, phone numbers, or other information concerning your spouse, children, or other relatives *not* employed by this company?

Will you provide names of your relatives, other than a spouse, already employed by this company?

What is the name and address of your nearest relative to be notified in case of an emergency?

What is the name and address of a person to be notified in case of an emergency?

Have you had any military experience?

What experience have you had in the armed forces, in the state militia, or in foreign military?

Will you submit proof of age? (before position is taken)

Will you submit a birth certificate or other proof of age? (after position is offered)

Will you submit a photograph of yourself? (before being hired)

Will you submit a photograph of yourself? (after being hired)

How tall are you, and what is your weight?

How tall are you and what is your weight? (acceptable only if employer can show that no employee with ineligible height or weight could do the work)

Additional illegal questions are those pertaining to race, color, past or current medical conditions not related to the specific job, your religious preferences, willingness to work on religious holidays, and disabilities. Other *legal* questions include inquiries into applicants' experience in organizations that is relevant to their potential job performance; inquiries about references (for example, "Who suggested that you apply for this position?" or asking for names of persons willing to provide proof and/or character references); inquiries about place and duration of residence; inquiries into applicants' academic, vocational, or professional education and schools attended; and inquiries into work experiences.

To summarize, interviewers are generally looking for certain attributes in an interviewee—namely, maturity, enthusiasm, creativity, and confidence, as well as thoughtfulness and intelligence. Do not underestimate the importance of careful preparation. Practicing your interviewing techniques in many situations can give you the experience you will need for your "dream job" interview. You want to make the most favorable impression possible. Be spontaneous, and direct and present your best self.

Follow-Up

Keep a running account of the date and place of all interviews and names, titles, and other important information about the interviewers. After the interviews, immediately write down your impressions of what was discussed. Record pertinent phone numbers, follow-up, and other information. Keep a careful record of every contact, as you may forget important details needed later. Exercise 8.1 asks you to answer some specific questions that will help you improve your interviewing skills.

Follow-up letters leave a favorable impression and can make a critical difference. In some cases, they can help you stand out if you had a successful interview. Include a brief note of appreciation plus a reminder of your special skills or qualities.

If you are invited for a second interview, continue to use the same approaches you have employed successfully to date. Another visit to the company will help you confirm your feeling about how good a fit the organization is for you as well as for them.

Interview Follow-Up

After an interview, record your answers to the following questions.

How has this compared to your past experience with job interviews?

_____

_____

_____

_____

What part of the job interview process do you need to work on the most? Why?

_____

_____

_____

_____

What specific steps can you take now to prepare for future interview situations?

_____

_____

_____

_____

Dealing With Rejection

In spite of your careful preparation and planning, you may not find a job right away. The average job search can take from six months to a year. This can be a discouraging experience, and you may start to put yourself down or feel inadequate. If this happens, take positive steps. Review your job-search approach and determine areas for improvement (e.g., resume, how you make contacts, interviewing). Ask yourself these questions:

Am I willing to take a lower-level position with the possibility of using it as a stepping-stone to a better one? (You risk selling yourself short, so be aware of future opportunities with the company rather than using it as an "out" for the present situation.)

Have I used all the resources available to me (e.g., untapped leads/referrals, alumni contacts)?

Do I have the resources to volunteer in a setting that would provide the experience I need?

Can I reach my career goal in other ways (e.g., shift my focus to another job area)?

Would further education enhance my prospects in my chosen career area?

Exercise 8.2 provides a means to record your thoughts about unsuccessful interviews.

EXERCISE 8.2　*Handling Rejection*

Answering the following questions may help you deal with rejection and plan some alternative strategies.

Have you ever been refused a job? If so, describe your reaction and what you would do differently *now* in that interview situation.

_____

_____

_____

If you have never been rejected from a job, how do you think you would react in that situation?

_____

_____

_____

Reexamining the requirements for future workers outlined in Chapter Three may give you some clues for exploring personal qualifications and possible new occupational environments. Finding a job requires patience, fortitude, and self-confidence. You eventually will find a position if you persevere and take a proactive approach.

Learning how to organize and carry out a job search is a complicated endeavor best started during your freshman year in college, but it is never too late to initiate the critical tasks involved in the process. You must be constantly aware of the resources available to help you reach your goal.

The skills you develop in the job-search process will carry over into the work world once you are hired. Managing a job-search campaign can help you appreciate the value of being organized, learning to write succinctly, learning how to do research and solve problems, learning how to communicate in a variety of situations, and building confidence in your abilities. These are attributes that many employers seek in an employee.

The suggestions below summarize the primary job-search components discussed in the last two chapters:

1. Start preparing for your job search as early as possible. You must accomplish many tasks before your senior year.
2. Employers prefer to interview and hire academically capable students over academically marginal ones.
3. Be active in work-related and campus activities that can provide the type of experiences you can use later to sell yourself.
4. Establish a resume worksheet on which you continue to record your goals, accomplishments, work experience, and other information during your college years; learn how to use Internet resources.
5. If possible, take part in a co-op or internship experience to strengthen your work record in a given field.
6. Prepare for interviews by obtaining information about prospective employers.
7. Practice your interviewing techniques in as many settings as you can, and ask for feedback. Your confidence and skill level will increase with each experience.
8. Follow up each contact with a letter of appreciation.

COMMITMENT To prepare for his interviews for a summer job, Jed went to several workshops offered by the career services office on his campus. He learned about the importance of preparing before the interview, because knowing as much as possible about the organization can help the applicant answer and ask questions. Jed took advantage of the opportunity to videotape himself in a mock interview with a professional employer. As he talked, he was surprised to see the little habits that were distracting.

The employer complimented Jed on his poise and confidence but offered several good suggestions for improvement. Jed also practiced his interviewing techniques on several family members and friends to be as well prepared as possible for the real thing.

When Maria went to her college's career services office to show her resume to a career counselor, she signed up for a workshop on interviewing skills. As soon as she feels confident, she will make an appointment with her current supervisor to try what she has learned. After exploring the possibilities within her company, Maria will decide whether to start the job-search process in earnest.

A friend has told her about some jobs she is qualified for in another company that is offering much higher salaries than what Maria is currently making. Maria must weigh the financial difference between a better salary at another company against the benefit of free tuition from her present employer. Maria feels confident that her newly acquired job-search skills will give her an advantage if and when she decides to look for a new job.

9. Check your progress regularly regarding whether what you are doing confirms your career goals.
10. Acquire appropriate campus, volunteer, and work experiences.
11. Be enthusiastic about selling yourself and your unique qualities. You're worth it!

Summary Checklist   CHAPTER 8

What I have learned

_____ I know how to generate job leads using specific contacts and resources.

_____ I have contacted my career-planning office or other resources for help in perfecting my job-search skills and have signed up for workshops or other help in developing these skills.

_____ I feel confident I know how to conduct myself in a job-interviewing situation before, during, and after the contact and have practiced in a simulated or real setting.

How I can use it

I know the steps in mounting a job search that will lead to interviews with a prospective employer and feel confident of my ability to market myself in an interview situation.

Where Do I Go From Here?

Nine

*T*hroughout this book you have examined many facets of career exploration and planning:

- You have learned about work in general and how your own perceptions of work will influence your choices.

- You have learned a process for career decision making and have become familiar with the knowledge, skills, attitudes, and behaviors necessary to progress through the process.

- You have examined and evaluated your personal strengths, such as the abilities, interests, values, and personality traits that make you a unique person.

- You have explored occupational areas and learned how to access and evaluate occupational information.

- You have identified educational options that lead to or complement possible occupational areas.

- You have glimpsed the workplace of the future and learned about the type of workers employers will be hiring.

- You have learned how to gain a psychological edge, which can increase your effectiveness as a worker.

- You have, perhaps, decided on a general or even a specific occupational or educational direction.

To help you determine where you are in the career decision-making process and where to go from here, consider the three methods in Exercises 9.1, 9.2, and 9.3. Exercise 9.1 will show you where you are at this point in your career planning. As a further check on where you need to go from here and to help you pull together everything you have learned, examine the flowchart in Figure 9.1. It can help you assemble the pieces of the larger picture into a coherent whole through a step-by-step process. It also suggests resources. Exercise 9.2 invites you to use Figure 9.1 in evaluating your career path thus far. Exercise 9.3 asks you to fill out the checklist below, then compare it to the one you completed in Exercise 1.6, Chapter One.

EXERCISE 9.1 *Method 1*

A Snapshot in the Career-Planning Process

Check where you are now in the career-planning process by revisiting the stages outlined in Chapter One, Table 1.2.

I believe I am now in the _____ phase of the career decision-making process because

_____

_____

_____

_____

EXERCISE 9.2 *Method 2*

Evaluating Career Planning

Referring to Figure 9.1, you will be able to trace your career journey to this point.

If you wish to retrace some steps, what are they?

_____

_____

_____

_____

What resources will you need in retracing these steps?

_____

_____

_____

_____

Flowchart: A path to a career decision. **FIGURE 9.1**

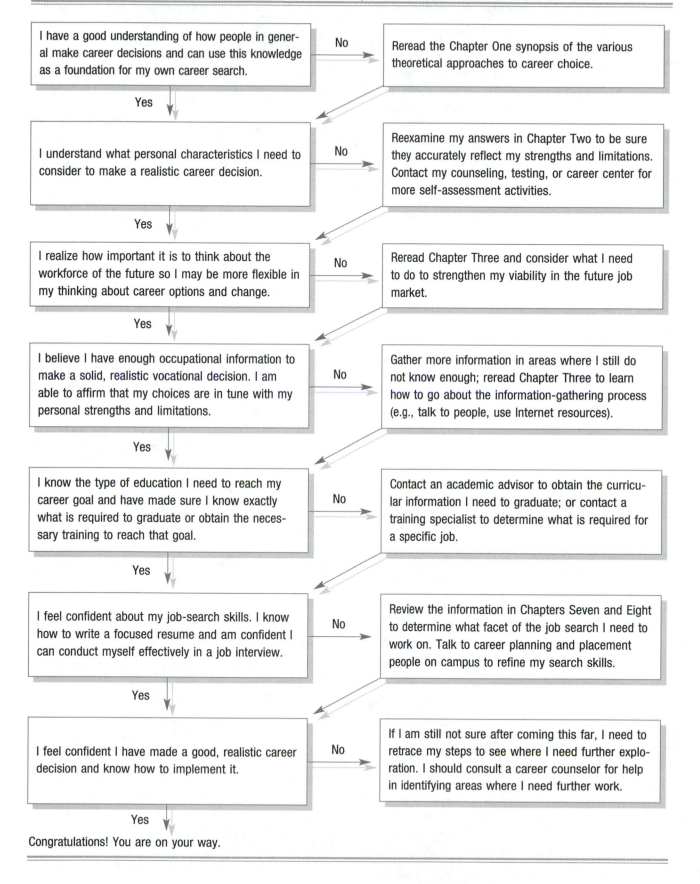

| I have a good understanding of how people in general make career decisions and can use this knowledge as a foundation for my own career search. | **No** → | Reread the Chapter One synopsis of the various theoretical approaches to career choice. |

Yes ↓

| I understand what personal characteristics I need to consider to make a realistic career decision. | **No** → | Reexamine my answers in Chapter Two to be sure they accurately reflect my strengths and limitations. Contact my counseling, testing, or career center for more self-assessment activities. |

Yes ↓

| I realize how important it is to think about the workforce of the future so I may be more flexible in my thinking about career options and change. | **No** → | Reread Chapter Three and consider what I need to do to strengthen my viability in the future job market. |

Yes ↓

| I believe I have enough occupational information to make a solid, realistic vocational decision. I am able to affirm that my choices are in tune with my personal strengths and limitations. | **No** → | Gather more information in areas where I still do not know enough; reread Chapter Three to learn how to go about the information-gathering process (e.g., talk to people, use Internet resources). |

Yes ↓

| I know the type of education I need to reach my career goal and have made sure I know exactly what is required to graduate or obtain the necessary training to reach that goal. | **No** → | Contact an academic advisor to obtain the curricular information I need to graduate; or contact a training specialist to determine what is required for a specific job. |

Yes ↓

| I feel confident about my job-search skills. I know how to write a focused resume and am confident I can conduct myself effectively in a job interview. | **No** → | Review the information in Chapters Seven and Eight to determine what facet of the job search I need to work on. Talk to career planning and placement people on campus to refine my search skills. |

Yes ↓

| I feel confident I have made a good, realistic career decision and know how to implement it. | **No** → | If I am still not sure after coming this far, I need to retrace my steps to see where I need further exploration. I should consult a career counselor for help in identifying areas where I need further work. |

Yes ↓

Congratulations! You are on your way.

Career Checklist Revisited

In Chapter One, Exercise 1.6, you checked the items in the following list that reflect the knowledge, skills, attitudes, and behaviors you wanted to learn about to make effective educational and vocational decisions.

Now check the same items below based on what you have actually learned, and compare your answers with those in Exercise 1.6. Are you confident you understand and can use this information now and in the future as you continue your career planning?

ONE: GETTING READY

_____   What is my attitude toward taking responsibility for becoming involved in my career planning?

_____   What does the career- and life-planning process mean?

_____   Where am I in the process, and did I productively use this book?

_____   How should I progress through the decision-making process so I can make realistic and satisfying choices?

TWO: WHAT DO I NEED TO KNOW ABOUT MYSELF?

_____   What are my perspectives on and attitudes toward work in general?

_____   What abilities do I currently possess for specific kinds of work tasks?

_____   What are my occupational interests?

_____   What is important to me in a job (e.g., income, type of people with whom I work, a job that allows me to be creative, to be self-employed)?

_____   How might my personality influence my occupational choices?

_____   How might my family background influence my occupational choices?

_____   How does my environment influence my career choices?

_____   Summarize what you still need to know about yourself:

THREE: WHAT DO I NEED TO KNOW ABOUT OCCUPATIONAL ALTERNATIVES?

_____   How can I locate the occupations that are realistic for me to explore? How can I narrow them down to a list of jobs that are realistic for me to explore?

_____   How will changes in the future workplace affect me?

_____   Where can I find important information regarding specific occupations (e.g., salaries, necessary skills, educational requirements, physical requirements, employment trends)?

_____   What are the best sources for finding occupational information (e.g., printed materials, computerized information, interviewing)?

_____   What work skills will I need to acquire for employment in the 21st century?

_____   How can I evaluate and use occupational information once I have found it?

_____   How can I apply information about occupations to what I know about my own strengths and limitations?

_____   Where will future job growth and opportunities exist?

_____   What occupational information do I still need?

FOUR: WHAT DO I NEED TO KNOW ABOUT EDUCATIONAL ALTERNATIVES?

_____ How can I select and/or confirm my choice of an academic major?

_____ How do certain majors match my abilities and interests?

_____ What educational background will I need for certain occupations (e.g., college, graduate or technical degree, apprenticeships)?

_____ What majors lead to specific occupational areas?

_____ Why don't certain occupations require specific college majors?

_____ How can I select courses to enhance the skills and knowledge I will need in the world or work?

_____ What can I do to test my ideas about a major (e.g., volunteer work, study abroad, experiential learning)?

_____ What educational information do I still need?

FIVE: HOW WILL I DECIDE?

_____ How can I learn to set short-term and long-term personal, educational, and occupational goals?

_____ Why is my personal style of making decisions important?

_____ Where am I in the decision-making process?

_____ How can I learn effective career decision-making skills?

_____ How can I use information about self, occupational, and educational options to generate alternatives?

_____ How do I implement a career decision I have made?

_____ How do I periodically reevaluate my decisions once I have lived with them for a while?

_____ If I am not confident about my decision-making ability, what do I need to do to improve it?

SIX: HOW WILL I GAIN A PSYCHOLOGICAL EDGE?

_____ What does it mean to gain the psychological edge in life and in the workplace?

_____ What specific behaviors do personally effective individuals practice?

_____ How can I adapt to change effectively?

_____ How can I learn to communicate effectively with my peers, instructors, and co-workers?

_____ What stressors am I experiencing?

_____ How should I manage stress?

_____ How do I apply a personal "Code of Ethics"?

_____ What work habits do I still need to improve?

SEVEN: HOW WILL I ADVANCE MY CAREER? THE JOB SEARCH AND RESUME WRITING

_____ What are the advantages of starting now to compile information about my experiences?

_____ What job-search skills do I need to learn now?

_____ How should I write a resume that will appeal to a prospective employer?

_____ How should I write an effective cover letter?

_____ How do I stay current on how to send resumes electronically?

EIGHT: AM I THE BEST CANDIDATE? JOB LEADS AND THE JOB INTERVIEW

_____ How can I generate job leads?

_____ What is the best way to prepare for a job interview?

_____ How can I make a good impression on a prospective employer during a job interview?

_____ What do I need to know about the difference between lawful and unlawful questions?

_____ Where do I learn about cyber-interviews and other electronic methods?

_____ How should I follow up after an interview?

NINE: WHERE DO I GO FROM HERE?

_____ Where am I now?

_____ What are my next steps?

Compare the items you checked on Exercise 1.6 with the same items you just checked. Have you accomplished what you intended?

_____ yes _____ no

If yes, you have made excellent progress. If no, what areas still need work?

_____

_____

_____

_____

_____

_____

As a final exercise, Exercise 9.4 is intended as your action plan for the future.

EXERCISE 9.4 *Action Planning*

Below, write some short- and long-term career goals you wish to accomplish in the future.

Short-term goals (to be accomplished within the next school term or year):

_____

_____

_____

_____

_____

_____

Long-term goals (to be accomplished in the next two or three years):

_____

_____

_____

_____

_____

_____

Compare these goals with the ones you set in Chapter Five. Have you met any of your original goals? Are they still the same?

Throughout this book we have emphasized that the career-planning process is a lifelong task. If you have made an educational and/or occupational decision at this point, congratulations!

If you have not yet decided, you now have an understanding of the knowledge, skills, attitudes, and behaviors needed to continue the search. By using the information and guidelines provided in this book, you can feel confident that you have the expertise to make personally satisfying career decisions now and in the future.

CASE STUDY   *Jed and Maria*

COMMITMENT Although Jed has made a choice of major and a general career direction, he knows that these are tentative decisions. Because he is still in his first year, many factors must come into play before his tentative goals can be fulfilled. Jed must earn a certain gradepoint average to apply for the education program at his college, as it is selective. He has decided, therefore, to concentrate on his coursework and has vowed to discipline himself to follow certain study habits.

Jed has set a schedule for studying, while at the same time realizing the importance of recreation and being with friends. He knows it is important to reach a balance in his life while enjoying the college experience. This is a new feeling for Jed, who usually took things as they came with little planning or thought about the future. He is confident in his ability to be flexible and open to change and looks forward to the rest of his experience.

Maria has just finished the last exercises in *Building Your Career*. She is pleased with what she has learned about herself and the computer job market. She has decided to pursue computer science as a major. She realizes that she must manage her non-work schedule carefully to include class and study time. She believes she has sharpened her decision-making skills and knows how to prepare a strong resume. Her action plan includes exploring new job possibilities within her present company and continuing to explore some specific skills she has identified that will be marketable in her current job or a new one.

References

Barner, R. (1994). *Lifeboat strategies: How to keep your career above water during tough times—or any time.* AMACOM.

Beck, A. T. (1976). *Cognitive therapy and the emotional disorders.* New York: Times Mirror.

Brown, D. (1984). Trait and factor theory. In D. Brown and L. Brooks (Eds.), *Career choice and development: Applying contemporary theories to practice.* San Francisco: Jossey-Bass.

Brown, D., and Brooks, L. (1991). *Career counseling techniques.* Boston: Allyn & Bacon.

Holland, J. L. (1985). *Making vocational choices: A theory of vocational personalities and work environments* (2d ed.). Englewood Cliffs, NJ: Prentice Hall.

Holmes, T. H., and Rahe, R. H. (1967). The social readjustment rating scale. *Journal of Psychosomatic Research,* 11(2), 213–218.

Hoppock, R. (1976). *Occupational information.* New York: McGraw-Hill.

Hotchkiss, L., and Borow, H. (1990). Sociological perspective on work and career development. In D. Brown and L. Brooks (Eds.), *Career choice and development: Applying contemporary theories to practice* (pp. 262–307). San Francisco: Jossey-Bass.

Johnson, D. W. (1987). *Human relations and your career.* Englewood Cliffs, NJ: Prentice Hall.

Johnson, and Coscarelli. (1983). *Manual for the decision making inventory.* Columbus, OH: Marathon Consulting and Press.

Johnston, W. and Packer, A. (1987). *Workforce 2000: Work and workers for the twenty-first century.* Indianapolis: Hudson Institute.

Lawrence. G. (1979). *People types and tiger stripes.* Gainesville, FL: Center for Applications of Psychological Type.

Meichenbaum, D. (1986). Cognitive behavior modification. In F. H. Kanfer and A. P. Goldstein (Eds.), *Helping people change: A textbook of methods* (pp. 346–380). New York: Pergamon Press.

Meister, J. C. (1994). *Corporate quality universities: Lessons in building a world-class workforce.* New York: Irwin Professional Publishing.

Myers, I. B. (1980). *Gifts differing.* Palo Alto, CA: Consulting Psychologists Press.

Myers, I. B., and McCaulley, M. H. (1985). *Manual: A guide to the development and use of the Myers-Briggs Type Indicator.* Palo Alto, CA: Consulting Psychologists Press.

Pitz, G. F., and Herren, V. A. (1980). An analysis of career decision making from the point of view of information-processing and decision theory. *Journal of Vocational Behavior,* 16, 320–346.

Sears, S. (1982). A definition of career guidance terms: A national vocational guidance association perspective. *Vocational Guidance Quarterly,* 31(2), 137–143.

Super, D. E. (1984). Career and life development. In D. Brown and L. Brooks (Eds.), *Career choice and development* (pp. 192–234). San Francisco: Jossey-Bass.

Tiedeman, D. V. & O'Hara, R. P. (1963). *Career development: Choice and adjustment.* New York: College Entrance Examination Board.

U. S. Department of Labor. (1999). *Occupational Outlook Handbook,* 2000–2001. Washington, DC: U.. S. Government Printing Office.

Index

2543